David M. Bergeron

David M. Bergeron

PRINTED FOR THE MALONE SOCIETY
BY VIVIAN RIDLER AT THE
UNIVERSITY PRESS
OXFORD

THE HOGGE HATH LOST
HIS PEARL
BY
ROBERT TAILOR

THE MALONE SOCIETY
REPRINTS
1967 (1972)

This edition of *The Hogge hath Lost his Pearl* has been prepared by D. F. McKenzie and checked by Arthur Brown and G. R. Proudfoot.

July 1971   G. R. PROUDFOOT

The Hogge hath Lost his Pearl was entered in the book of copies at Stationers' Hall on 23 May 1614:

Rich: Redmer. Entred for his Coppie vnder the hand$ of m^r Taverno^r Sr George Bucke and m^r ffeild warden a play booke called Hogge hath lost his pearle. vj^d

[Register C, fol. 251^a: Greg, *Bibliography of the Drama*, i. 28]

Greg notes that the double licence is unusual and comments: 'There appears to have been some hesitation about accepting Buc's licence unless supported by a regular corrector of the press' (*Bibliography*, iv. 1682). This precaution was doubtless taken because the play had given offence when first produced.

Redmer's edition appeared in 1614 and collates: 4°, A–H⁴; 32 leaves, unpaged; \$3 signed (—A1, A2, and H3). Its contents run: A1 and A1ᵛ, blank; A2, title (verso blank); A3, the prologue; A4, the actors' names; B1, text; on H3, '*FINIS.*'; H3ᵛ, blank; H4, epilogue (verso blank). The text is printed in roman to a normal page depth of 38 lines (39 on C3ᵛ, D4, D4ᵛ, E3, G3ᵛ; 20 lines = *c.* 81 mm.) with italic for the prologue, epilogue, running titles, speech headings, proper names, and stage directions. Catchwords are normal throughout except for D2ᵛ, E3, and E3ᵛ, where the catchword is variant, and E4ᵛ, where it is omitted; the catchword on B1 gives a speech prefix omitted on B1ᵛ; that on H2ᵛ erroneously follows the text in omitting a speech prefix. The play is divided into acts but not into scenes (except for the opening one, marked 'Actus primi Scena prima.'). Scene numbers have been added in the present reprint.

Running titles suggest that most of the quarto was printed with two skeleton formes; a third was evidently made up for E(i) and a fourth constructed from elements of I and II to print and perfect sheet H. Forme I printed B(o), B(i), C(o), D(o), F(i), G(o); forme II printed C(i), D(i), E(o), F(o), G(i); forme III printed E(i); forme IV printed H(o), H(i). Slight changes in spelling, punctuation, and spacing occurred within skeleton formes I and II as they were reimposed for successive sheets.

The printer of the 1614 quarto was John Beale. The title-page ornament, a mask with shield and leaves, may be found also on A1 of *S.T.C.* 22395, Sheldon's *The First Sermon* (1612), printed by 'I. B.' The headpiece on A3 is a common cast ornament with vase, scrolls, and birds, but this example shows a slight crack running through the right lower bulge of the vase; it may be seen also on a1, B2, and L3 of *S.T.C.* 15268, *Lathams Falconry*, part I of which (1615) gives Beale's initials, part II (1618) his full name, and on A1 and A1ᵛ of *S.T.C.* 23047a, John Speed's *Historie of Great Britaine* (1623), which was printed by Beale.

Not much is known about the author, Robert Tailor. He contributed commendatory verses to *The Nipping or Snipping of Abuses*, by John Taylor, published in 1614 (*S.T.C.* 23779—entered at Stationers' Hall 7 December 1613), in which he speaks of his own work as of less repute than that of the water poet. There is no evidence identifying him with the Robert Tailour whose five-part settings of the psalms were included in Sir Edwin Sandys's *Sacred Hymns* of 1615 (*S.T.C.* 21723).

On the play itself, however, there is a contemporary comment by Sir Henry Wotton who wrote in a letter to Sir Edmund Bacon:

...On *Sunday* last at night, and no longer; some sixteen Apprentices (of what sort you shall guess by the rest of the story) having secretly learnt a new Play without book, intituled, *The Hog hath lost his Pearl*; took up the White-Fryers for their Theatre: and having invited thither (as it should seem) rather their Mistresses then their Masters; who were all to enter *per buletini* for a note of distinction from ordinary Comedians towards the end of the Play, the Sheriffs (who by chance had heard of it) came in (as they say) and carried some six or seven of them to perform the last act at *Bridewel*; the rest are fled. Now it is strange to hear how sharp-witted the City is, for they will needs have Sir *John Swinerton* the Lord *Maior* be meant by the *Hog*, and the late Lord Treasurer [Lord Salisbury] by the *Pearl*. And now let me bid you good night, from my Chamber in *King-ſtreet* this *Tuesday*, at Eleven of the night,

Your faithfullest to serve you,
HENRY WOTTON.

[*Letters of Sir Henry Wotton to Sir Edmund Bacon.* (London, 1661), 155–6.]

The letter is only dated 'Tuesday', 1612–13, but refers earlier to the departure of the King, which was 22 February 1613, as on the previous day. The date of the performance referred to would therefore have been 21 February 1613.

The reasons for linking Sir John Swinnerton with the play have been most fully discussed by Miss Evelyn May Albright in 'A Stage Cartoon of the Mayor of London in 1613', in *The Manly Anniversary Studies in Language and Literature* (Chicago, 1923), pp. 113–26. Miss Albright establishes that Swinnerton had long competed with the powerful company of farmers of the great customs for certain lucrative grants of patents on wines. In 1607, with only partial success, he had attacked the validity of his competitors' patent and attempted to secure a fresh grant to himself; and in 1612–13, the year of his mayoralty, he used the advantages of his office to try to persuade the King to annul the grants to the farmers of the custom. In a letter of 3 September 1612, written in support of Swinnerton, the Earl of Northampton declared that the patentees were so angry at their tricks being discovered that they had attacked Sir John Swinnerton's character; and in a direct application to the King on 8 October, Northampton noted the late Lord Treasurer's opposition to Swinnerton's claims. John Chamberlaine, writing to Sir Ralph Winwood on 9 January 1613, records that

A Day or two before *Christmas* [1612], the King himself gave a Hearing to a Controversie 'twixt the Farmers of the Customes and Sir *John Swinerton* now Lord-Mayor, who accused them of defrauding the King yearly of 70000*l*; but when it came to Proof it could not be made good; so that they went away acquitted, and he not much condemned for seeking the King's Benefit.

[*Memorials of Affairs of State*. 3 vols. (London, 1725), iii. 422.]

On 5 January 1613 Swinnerton was himself charged with fraudulent conduct of the farm of sweet wines: first, in exacting usurious rents from the new imposts, which were in mortgage to the city of London; and second, in using his position as mayor to prevent the redemption of those mortgages (cf. lines 71, 100, 468, 712, 1752, 1957 and *S.P.D. 1611–18*, p. 166). The following month Tailor's play was performed.

The application to Swinnerton sufficiently explains the sheriffs' concern, the disavowals of the prologue and the double licence. It is less easy to accept that the 'pearle' was Salisbury, the late Lord Treasurer, who had died on 24 May 1612. The pearl may have been simply a convenient symbol for Swinnerton's highest aspiration —the riches to be won from the farm of certain fermented wines which he hoped to add to his own limited patent (although, as the play enacts it, his command of the 'powerful spirits' which promised such rewards was to prove illusory and his loss commensurate with his greed). Nevertheless, the 'orient pearle' of the play (line 1739) may also have had a more specific topicality, again pointing to Swinnerton, for on the morning of 14 February 1613, one week before the play was performed,

The City of *London* (that with high magnificence had feasted the Prince *Palatine*, and his *Noble* Retinue) presented to the *fair Bride* a Chain of *Oriental Pearl*, by the hand of the Lord *Mayor*, and *Aldermen* . . .
  [Arthur Wilson, *The History of Great Britain, being the Life and Reign of King James I* (1653), p. 64.]

John Chamberlaine, in a letter to Winwood of 3 November 1612, additionally notes that after seeing the show in Cheapside the Count Palatine and his company

went to *Guildhall*, and were there plentifully feasted and wellcomed by Sir *John Swinerton* the new Lord Mayor, and presented toward the end of Dinner with a fair standing Cup, a fair Bason and Ewre, with two large Livery Pots, weighing together toward 1200 Ounces (to the Value of almost 500*l.*) in the Name of the City.

[*Memorials of Affairs of State*, iii. 407.]

Wotton says that the play was 'secretly learnt . . . without book', and it may be that the text as 'divers times publikely acted' and subsequently licensed and printed, has been recast. As it stands the play reads less like personal satire than general burlesque. The theatrical banter in Act I and stage effects in Act V, the resort to stock routines of substitution and disguise, and the extremities of sententiousness, pastoral romance, and farce suggested such an intention. Fleay conjectured that Haddit might be identified with Dekker (*A Biographical Chronicle of the English Drama*, 2 vols. (London, 1891), ii. 256–7). But if Dekker is alluded to at all, it is more generally. He had written the show *Troia-Nova Triumphans* to mark Swinnerton's inauguration on 29 October 1612; and Tailor's play shows many superficial similarities to Dekker's *If this be not a Good Play, the Devil is in it* (1612). It would be unsafe to press the case further. W. Smith's *The Hector of Germany* (1615), acted at the Red Bull and the Curtain by a company of young men of the city, perhaps did something to answer the effects of *The Hogge hath Lost his Pearl*: it was dedicated 'To the Right Worshipfull, the Great Fauourer of the Muses, Syr John Swinnerton Knight, sometimes Lord Mayor of this honourable Cittie of London'.

The Hogge hath Lost his Pearl was included in the several editions of Robert Dodsley's *A Select Collection of Old Plays*: Dodsley's of 1744 (vol. 3); Reed's of 1780 (vol. 6); Collier's of 1825–8 (vol. 6); and Hazlitt's of 1874–6 (vol. 11). It was also included in Walter Scott's *The Ancient British Drama* (vol. 3) in 1810.

The present reprint is based on photographs of the quarto at the Shakespeare Centre, Stratford-upon-Avon. It is one of the two complete copies to contain in their corrected states all the variant formes so far noted. The plates are reproduced from photographs of the copy in the Guildhall Library. The thanks of the Society are due to the authorities mentioned for permission to use the copies in their care.

List of Variant Readings

There are at least twenty copies extant of the 1614 quarto of this play, all of which have been collated for purposes of the present reprint. Their locations, and the symbols used to designate them, are as follows:

Bodleian Library (Malone)	B
British Museum (644.f.64)	BM1
British Museum (162.e.8)	BM2
Boston Public Library	BPL
Eton College Library	E
Folger Shakespeare Library	F1
Folger Shakespeare Library	F2
Guildhall Library, London	G
Harvard University Library	H
Henry E. Huntington Library	HH
Library of Congress	LC
National Library of Scotland (Bute)	NLS
New York Public Library (Arents)	NYPL
Pepys Library, Magdalene College, Cambridge	P
Shakespeare Centre, Stratford-upon-Avon	S
University of London Library	UL
Victoria and Albert Museum (Dyce)	VA
Winchester College Library	W
Worcester College Oxford	WOR
Yale University Library	Y

Most copies lack the initial blank leaf (A1); B and WOR want H4, and W the whole of sheet H.

Variant readings occur in the following five formes:

A (outer): corrected state in B, BM1, BM2, BPL, E, G, H, HH, LC, NLS, NYPL, P, S, UL, W, WOR, Y; uncorrected state in F1, F2, VA.

B (outer): this forme was corrected in three stages: (i) in BPL, F2, NYPL, Y, correcting only line 162 on B3; (ii) in F1, also correcting B4^v; (iii) in B, E, G, NLS, S, UL, VA, W, WOR, also correcting lines 136, 141–2 on B3; uncorrected state in BM1, BM2, H, HH, LC, P.

D (outer): corrected state in B, BM1, BM2, BPL, F1, F2, G, H, HH, LC, NYPL, P, S, UL, VA, W, WOR, Y; uncorrected state in E, NLS.

E (outer): corrected state in B, BM1, BM2, BPL, E, F1, F2, H, HH, LC, NLS, NYPL, P, S, UL, VA, W, WOR, Y; uncorrected state in G.

E (inner): corrected state in B, BM1, BM2, BPL, E, F1, F2, H, HH, LC, NLS, NYPL, P, S, UL, VA, W, WOR, Y; uncorrected state in G.

In the following list of variant readings the reading of the corrected forme, and therefore of this reprint, is given first.

A3	5	*loſt labour,*] *loſt, labour*
	20	*ſwines fleſh*] *ſwine fleſh*
	22	*queſtionleſſeit*] *queſteonleſſe it*
B3	136	*Who buyes my fowre ropes of hard Onions*] who buyes my fowre ropes of hard Onions
	141	dark] darke
	141	you] om.
	141–2	cõ-/mõly] com-/monly
	142	are] om.
	142	&] and
	162	Phiſicke] Phicke
B4ᵛ	251	affection] effection
	267	loue,] loue
	267	you] om.
	273	thither] thether
	274	flight,] flight
D2ᵛ	738	reignes] reanes
D3	763	damn'd] damnd
	770	breeds] breads
E3	1054	goodneſſe] goopneſſe
	1082	your] eour
	1083	inherite hea-] inherite
	c.w.	uen] heauen
E3ᵛ	1120	taſt] taſte
	1120	gentlem.] gen-/tlemen.
	1120	the line is more deeply indented in its uncorrected state.

1121	*Li.* Pray begin, wele pleadge you ſir.] om.
c.w.	*Pe.*] *Li.*
E4ᵛ 1183	friendſhip,] friendſhip
1187	tell] om.
1191	it,] it

In addition to these corrections the variant states of outer D and E reveal the following minor variations.

D3	765	beheld] the first e is clear only in the uncorrected state.
E4ᵛ	1160	is] the s is well above the line in the uncorrected state but tends to fall below it in the corrected state.

These further variants seem to bear no relation to press correction.

B4	214	promiſty ou] 'promi ſtyou' in some copies.
C1ᵛ	341	stage direction further to left in some copies.
E3ᵛ	1084	uen ant] some copies read 'uenant'.

LIST OF IRREGULAR AND DOUBTFUL READINGS

In the following list notice is only seldom taken of anomalous or erroneous spacing, and spacing material which has inadvertently printed is not recorded at all. No punctuation mark of any kind appears after the abbreviated speech-prefixes at 85, 118, 391, 1103, 1570; nor after the speeches ending at 118, 443, 494, 990, 1911, and the sentence ending at 1240. A comma instead of a full point occurs after the abbreviated speech-prefixes at 61, 84, 150, 343, 421, 891, 1082, 1095, 1148, 1793; and after the speeches (or occasionally sentences within them) ending at 47, 60, 83, 84, 89, 154, 214, 234, 286, 342, 343, 349, 351, 383, 385, 409, 575, 634, 671, 677, 685, 892, 904, 1041, 1075, 1086, 1107, 1111, 1122, 1128. A colon is used after the speeches ending at 277, 392, 394, 395, 435, 1350; and a black-letter colon appears to have been used at 87, 614, 1385. There is a turned full point at the end of 776. No punctuation is found after the stage directions at 107, 112, 150, 262, 352, 407, 435, 851; those at 341, 449, 1098 have only a comma after them. The speech prefix *Echo* is erroneously printed and punctuated as part of Echo's speeches at 1350, 1353, 1356, 1359, 1365, 1367, 1368.

The first lines of speeches, with their prefixes, are normally indented, but slight variations in the amount of indentation occur in full lines. The two lines from a song at 151–2 are indented, but those at 219–20 are not, nor is the motto at 808 or the couplet at 1106–7. Lightfoote's addresses to Ascarion at 1661–3 and to Bazon at 1706–9 are set in italic as stage directions.

A stop-press variant not recorded above is the transfer of the stage direction '*the Player appeares.*' on G3 from 1664 (so UL) to the centre of 1663 (so G); from there it is again moved slightly to the right (all other copies). In the headline on G3ᵛ, the word '*pearle.*' begins to move right in UL ('*his pear le.*'); in BM1, G, HH, LC, P, W, the whole word has moved across ('*his pearle.*'); in all other copies the headline is normal. Errors in the setting of the headline occur as follows: *Hoogge* B2C3; *loſthis* B3ᵛ4ᵛ, CDE2ᵛ, FH1ᵛ2ᵛ; *pearle,* CD1ᵛ.

There is some evidence that I and W were occasionally in short supply: I and *I*, W and VV are intermixed at many points throughout the quarto, but C1ᵛ–3, F1ᵛ–2ᵛ and G3ᵛ show a predominance of the substitute forms. A few readings are cited from notes or alterations made in manuscript in B (Malone 169, which served as copy for Dodsley's edition of 1744), in VA, and in BM2, where these seem to give probable emendations. The alterations in B appear to have been made by Dodsley himself; they may be compared with those in BM. C.34.e.11, a copy of *The Revenger's Tragedy* (1607): see A. T. Brissenden, 'Dodsley's Copy-Text for *The Revenger's Tragedy* in his *Select Collection*', *The Library*, 5th ser. xix (1964), 254–8.

Prologue

  10 *define*] B (Ms) reads *devine*

Text

  24 lacks speech prefix for *Lightfoote: see* B1 *c.w.; Li.* Then

  26 with (*possibly* wlth *in* F1, VA)

  29 inro

  37 found (f *resembles* ſ *in some copies*)

  44 tente] B (Ms) *reads* Tenant

  65 fortune.] . *not inking in most copies*

  66 That'ſt] Hazlitt *reads* Thou'st (*read* Th'ast)

  80 loueme

  97 deendien] VA (Ms) *reads* dee intend (*see* 422, d'ee intend)

111 wordsand

114 *Had.*] . *not inking in most copies*

118 (*aurora*] (*turned*

126 althouh

153 eome

156 ſhcwes

172 *Pla.*] *a* not inking in most copies

185 ſhotly (*read* ſhortly)

203, 206 fully indented

216 mnſt

238 *At.* (read *Al.*)

266   *outs* (? read *oute*)
289   lacks speech prefix *Ca.*
292   Man] B (Ms) *reads* For Man
308   Icannot
332   two ſtrictt
346   no aside marked
371   gaine.
373   hides] Hazlitt *reads* hies
387   nights] i *resembles* l *in some copies*
424   Faithts (*read* Faith'ts; *see* 860)
434   oureies
439   priſe.
440   muchof
441   not be mixted (*read* not to be mixed)
445   diſtruſt] Dodsley *reads* discuss'd
457   *ſeruitude*
461   youſir
474   chiſtendome
485   wilde fire (*six copies show traces of possible -*)
495   Moreouer] B (Ms) *reads* Morrow
524   aſide (*s.d. set as part of text*)
533   Intruth
555   al's, one
598   apreparatiue
599   notice (*perhaps with turned* i *in* BPL, NYPL; i *un-dotted in all other copies*)
619–20   thee me,/ As (? *read* me,/ Thee, as)
640   Not] B (Ms) *reads* They
642   enioyers, can
665   though (*read* thought)

678   *Fa.*] BM2 *Fa,* (*probably as result of poor inking or damage to type*)
685   doesſcratch
689   *Haddid*
721   of them] B (Ms) *reads* from (? *read* off the)
737   andthough
D2ᵛ   c.w. Ɛnte (S, E have possible traces of damaged *r*)
743   all afflicted] Dodsley *reads* all-afflicting
746   Should (S *turned*)
751   pri'zd
755   pleaſiing
756   genle
761   ſimpathi'zd
776   wife.] . *turned*
785   portion] B *and* VA (Ms) *read* potion
796   backe] Dodsley *reads* barks (*read* barke)
844   knowlede
890   ſought, for
971   ſend] ſ *resembles* f *in some copies*
987   iuſtly (l *not visible in* BM2)
1019   yous (*read* your)
1041–4   these lines, and 1078–83, i.e. those at the head of the outer forme of sheet E, are slurred in NYPL.
1043   *Exennt.*
1058–9   will/ will
1059   away (*read* a way)
1078–83   see note on 1041–4
1079–80   no aside marked
1098   Come] B (Ms) reads &

1122 my hand in (? *read* is my hand
       in *or* my hand is in)
1130 *Lighfoote*
1131 *welthy*
1136 Lords (*read* Lorde)
1139 beſworne
1170 feteh
1194 blacke ſinne (? *read* blacke a
       ſinne)
E4ᵛ   c.w. omitted
1201 *rising space resembles ! after
       from*
1214 wan (? *read* won)
1216 His] VA (Ms) *reads* Her
       (? *read* Her *or* This)
1224 taſte] B *and* VA (Ms) *and*
       Collier *read* cast
1224 vale of death] VA (Ms) *and*
       Collier *read* veil of death
1224 on] VA (Ms) *reads* in
1230 vnexpc̈ted
1236 them brats] VA (Ms) *reads*
       th'embrace
1250 by her, thought him
1252 heynous, crime
1263 wrong'd (' *turned*)
1265 eauſ'd
1280 To] VA (Ms) *reads* So *or*
       Do
1289 withall (*read* with all)
1304 willl
1308 no speech prefix for *Maria*;
       B (Ms) reads *Ma*:
1318 helpe (? *read* helpe me)
1335 with] B (Ms) *reads* which
1350 *Echo, Echo, Echo.* (read *Echo.
       Echo Echo.*; see introduc-
       tion, p. xii)

1366, 1369   lack speech prefix for
       Carracus and are not indented
1371 Conncellors
1372 refolue
1408 orer-ul'd
1455 ttee (*read* tree)
1462 ſaid (*read* ſad)
1474 vnſauowry
1481 *Albert*] VA (Ms) adds *&
       Carracus*
1483 ſeeemes
1499 you (*read* yon)
1502 to,
1532 and claſpe] B (Ms) *reads* he
       clasps
1535 we infold] B *and* VA (Ms)
       read we may infold
1573 ſirſt
1576 vety
1589 forth] B (Ms) *reads* fro⟨m
1594 Hir (*read* His)
1605 yallow
1627 *Elizum*
1628 *Acharon*
1688 mortall be?
1696 apletree (*read* axletree)
1701 Poſteth] B (Ms) *reads* Posting
1704 *Bazan*
1706 *did'ſt* (? read *doſt*)
1710 VA (Ms) adds *Hadit like*
       before s.d.
1711 *not indented*
1715 'Ime rai'sd
1738 weſtward (*read* eaſtward)
1742 ſhadewill
1749 I] B *and* VA (Ms) *read* Or
1749 ſuit] B (Ms) *reads* Shade
1750 *Lo.* (read *Li.*)

1750–60 no aside marked
1754   the (e *damaged*)
1755   friends (s *damaged*)
1760   VA (Ms) adds s.d. *Exit*
1780   *Lighfoote*
1826   Lords (*read* Lorde)
1827   Lord (r *turned*)
1841, 1846 *Pe.* (read *Pri.*)
1846   by our (*read* by your)
1870   heteafter
1880   VA and BM2 (Ms) add speech
        prefix *Car.*
1886   proofe
1892   Hogge (*roman for italic*)
1893   *Ho.*] VA (Ms) reads *Lo.*
1918   ceafe (i.e. *seize*)

1923   recount (*read* recount it)
1928   Hogge (*roman for italic*)
1936   as mad affright,] B (Ms)
        reads affrighted, ; Dodsley
        reads amaz'd, affrighted,
H2ᵛ   c.w. omits speech prefix for
        Haddit; added in VA (Ms)
1951   VA and BM2 (Ms) add
        speech prefix *Had.*
1968   wcele
1971   repent nt] LC, VA *read*
        repentant ; *the a is added in
        manuscript*

Epilogue
  13   *applouded*

THE
HOGGE
HATH LOST
HIS *PEARLE*.

A Comedy.

DIVERS TIMES
Publikely acted, by certaine
LONDON *Prentices*.

By ROBERT TAILOR.

LONDON,
Printed for *Richard Redmer*, and are to
be folde at the Weft dore of *Paules*
at the figne of the Starre.
1614

TITLE-PAGE, A2 RECTO (GUILDHALL)

THE
PROLOGVE.

OVR long time rumor'd *Hogge*, so often crost
By vnexpected accidents, and tost
From one house to another, still deceiuing
Many mens expectations, and bequeathing
To some lost labour, is at length got loose,
Leauing his seruile yoake-sticke to the goose,
Hath a Knights licence, and may raunge at pleasure,
Spight of all those that enuy our *Hogges* treasure:
And thus much let me tell you, that our *Swyne*
Is not as diuers Crittickes did define,
Grunting at State affaires, or inuecting
Much, at our Citty vices; no, nor detecting
The pride, or fraude, in it, but were it now
He had his first birth, wit should teach him how
To taxe these times abuses, and tell some
How ill they did in running oft from home,
For to preuent (O men more hard then flint)
A matter that shall laugh at them in print:
Once to proceede in this play we were mindlesse,
Thinking we liu'd mongst *Iewes* that lou'd no swines flesh:
But now that troubles past, if it deserue a hisse,
(As questionlesseie wil through our amisse,)

A 3

Let

PROLOGUE, A3 RECTO (GUILDHALL)

THE PROLOGVE.

Let it be fauoured by your gentle sufferance,
Wise-men are still indu'd with patience,
Wee are not halfe so skild as strowling Players,
Who could not please heere as at Country faiers,
we may be pelted off for ought we know,
With apples, egges, or stones from thence belowe;
In which weele craue your friendship if we may,
And you shall haue a daunce worth all the play,
And if it proue so happy as to please,
Weele say tis fortunate like Pericles.

PROLOGUE, A3 VERSO (GUILDHALL)

THE ACTORS
NAMES.

Old lord VVealthy.
Young lord his fonne.
Maria *his daughter.*

Carracus *and* Albert,
two Gentlemen, nere friends.

Lightfoote *a country Gentlem.*
Haddit *a youthfull Gallant.*

Hogge *a Vfurer.*
Rebecka *his daughter.*
Peter *Seruitude his man.*

Atlas

The Actors names.

Atlas *a Torter.*

A Priest.

A Player.

A Seruingman.

A Nurse.

THE
HOGGE HATH
loſt his Pearle.

Aɗus primi Scena prima.

Enter Lightfoote *a coūntry gentleman paſsing oʋer the ſtage*
and knocks at the other dore.

Lightfoote.

Oe, Whoſe within here?   *Enter Atlas a Porter*
 At. Ha ye any mony to pay you knock with
ſuch authority ſir?
 Li. What if I haue not, may not a man knock
without money ſir?

 At. Seldome, women and Seriaunts they will not put it vp
ſo ſir.

 Li. How ſay you by that ſir, but I prethee is not this one *At-*
las his houſe a Porter?

 At. I am the rent payer thereof.
 Li. In good time ſir.
 At. Not in good time, neither ſir, for I am behinde with my
Land-lord a yeere and three quarters at leaſt.

 Li. Now if a man would giue but obſeruance to this fel-
lowes prating, a would weary his eares ſooner then a Barber,
dee heare ſir, lies there not one Haddit a gentleman at this
houſe?

 At. Here lies ſuch a gentleman ir whoſe cloathes (were
they not greaſie) would beſpeake him ſo.

       B   *Li.* Then

EPILOGVE.

NOW expectation hath at full receiued
what we late promised, if in ought we haue pleased,
Tis all vve sought to accomplish, and much more
Then our vveake merrit dares to attribute
Vnto it selfe, till you vouchsafe to dayne
In your kinde censure, so to gratifie
Our triuiall labours : ————
If it hath pleased the iudiciall eare,
Wee haue our Authors wish, and void of feare
Dare ignorant men, to shew their worst of hate.
It not detracts, but adds vnto that state
Where desert florisheth.
Weele rest applouded in their derogation,
Though with an hisse they crowne that confirmation:
For this our Author saith, ift proue distastfull,
He onely grieues you spent two houres so wast-full:
But if it like, and you affect his pen,
You may commaund it when you please agen.

EPILOGUE, H4 RECTO (GUILDHALL)

THE
HOGGE
HATH LOST
HIS *PEARLE*.

A Comedy.

DIVERS TIMES
Publikely acted, by certaine
LONDON *Prentices*.

By ROBERT TAILOR.

LONDON,
Printed for *Richard Redmer*, and are to
be folde at the Weft-dore of *Paules*
at the figne of the Starre.
1614.

THE
PROLOGVE.

O*VR long time rumor'd Hogge, so often croſt*
By vnexpected accidents, and toſt
From one houſe to another, ſtill deceiuing
Many mens expectations, and bequeathing
To ſome loſt labour, is at length got looſe,
Leauing his ſeruile yoake-ſticke to the gooſe,
Hath a Knights licence, and may raunge at pleaſure,
Spight of all thoſe that enuy our Hogges treaſure:
And thus much let me tell you, that our Swyne
Is not as diuers Crittickes did define,   10
Grunting at State affaires, or inuecting
Much, at our Citty vices; no, nor detecting
The pride, or fraude, in it, but were it now
He had his firſt birth, wit ſhould teach him how
To taxe theſe times abuſes, and tell ſome
How ill they did in running oft from home,
For to preuent (O men more hard then flint)
A matter that ſhall laugh at them in print:
Once to proceede in this play we were mindleſſe,
Thinking we liu'd mongſt Iewes that lou'd no ſwines fleſh: 20
But now that troubles paſt, if it deſerue a hiſſe,
(As queſtionleſſe it wil through our amiſſe,)

A 3

Let

THE PROLOGVE.

Let it be fauoured by your gentle sufferance,
Wise-men are still indu'd with patience,
Wee are not halfe so skild as strowling Players,
Who could not please heere as at Country faiers,
We may be pelted off for ought we know,
With apples, egges, or stones from thence belowe;
In which weele craue your friendship if we may,
₃₀ *And you shall haue a daunce worth all the play,*
And if it proue so happy as to please,
Weele say tis fortunate like Pericles.

THE ACTORS
NAMES.

Old lord VVealthy.
Young lord his fonne.
Maria *his daughter.*

Carracus *and* Albert,
  two Gentlemen, *nere friends.*

Lightfoote *a country* Gentlem.
Haddit *a youthfull* Gallant.

Hogge *a* Vfurer.
Rebecka *his daughter.*
Peter *Seruitude his man.*

Atlas

The Actors names.

Atlas *a Porter*.

A Prieſt.

A Player.

A Seruingman.

A Nurſe.

THE
HOGGE HATH
loſt his Pearle.

Actus primi Scena prima.

Enter Lightfoote *a country gentleman paſsing ouer the ſtage*
and knocks at the other dore.

Lightfoote.

Oe, Whoſe within here? *Enter Atlas a Porter*
 At. Ha ye any mony to pay you knock with
ſuch authority ſir?
 Li. What if I haue not, may not a man knock
without money ſir?

At. Seldome, women and Seriaunts they will not put it vp 10
ſo ſir.

Li. How ſay you by that ſir, but I prethee is not this one *At-*
las his houſe a Porter?

At. I am the rent payer thereof.

Li. In good time ſir.

At. Not in good time, neither ſir, for I am behinde with my
Land-lord a yeere and three quarters at leaſt.

Li. Now if a man would giue but obſeruance to this fel-
lowes prating, a would weary his eares ſooner then a Barber,
dee heare ſir, lies there not one Haddit a gentleman at this 20
houſe?

At. Here lies ſuch a gentleman ſir whoſe cloathes (were
they not greaſie) would beſpeake him ſo.

B

Li. Then

Then I pray ſir when your leaſure ſhall permit, that you would vouchſafe to helpe me to the ſpeech of him.

At. We muſt firſt craue your oath, ſir that you come not with intent to moleſt, perturbe, or indaunger him, for he is a gent. whom it hath pleaſed fortune to make her tennis ball of, and therefore ſubiect to be ſtrucke by euery foole inro haſſard.

30   *Li.* In that I commend thy care of him, for which friendſhip heres a ſlight reward, tell him a Country man of his, one *Light-foote* is here, and will not any way diſpaire of his ſafetie.

At. With all reſpect Sir, pray commaund my houſe.

Exit Atlas.

Li. So, now I ſhall haue a ſight of my Coſen gallant, he that hath conſumed 800. pound a yeare, in as few yeares, as he hath eares on his head : He that was wont neuer to be found without 3, or 4, paire of red breeches, running before his horſe, or coach. He that at a meale, hath had more ſeuerall kindes, then I thinke
40 the Arke conteyn'd : He that was admir'd by niters, for his robes of gallantry, and was indeed all that an elder brother might be, prodigall, yet he, whoſe vnthriftineſſe kept many a houſe, is now glad to keepe houſe in a houſe, that keepes him the poore tente of a porter, and ſee his appearance, Ile ſeeme ſtrange to him.

Enter Haddit in poore Array.

Had. Coſen *Lightfoote* how doſt, welcome to the City,

Li. Who cals me Coſen, wheres my Coſen Haddit, hees ſurely putting on ſome rich apparell, for me to ſee him in. I ha
50 bin thinking al the way I came vp, how much his company will Credit me.

Had. My name is Haddit Sir, and your kineſman, if parents may be truſted, and therefore you may pleaſe to know me bet-ter, when you ſee me next.

Li. I prethee fellow ſtay, is it poſſible thou ſhouldſt be he, why he was the generous ſparke of mens admiration.

Had. I am that ſparke Sir, though now rak't vp in aſhes, Yet when it pleaſeth fortunes chops to blow

ſome

Some gentler gale vpon me, I may then,
From forth of embers riſe and ſhine agen,   60
   Li, O by your verſifying I know you now ſir, how doſt, I
knew thee not at firſt, thart very much altered.
   Had. Faith and ſo I am, exceeding much ſince you ſawe me
laſt, about eight hundred pound a yeere; but let it paſſe, for paſſage carried away the moſt part of it, a plague of fortune.
   Li. That'ſt more neede to pray to fortune then curſe her,
ſhe may be kind to thee when thou art penitent, but that I feare
will be neuer.
   Had. O no, if ſhe be a woman, ſheele euer loue thoſe that
hate her, but cozen thou art thy fathers firſt-borne, helpe me 70
but to ſome meanes, and Ile redeeme my mortgag'd lands with
a wench to boote.
   Li. As how I pray thee?
   Ha. Marry thus, *Hogge* the Vſurer hath one only daughter.
   Li. Is his name *Hogge*, it fits him exceeding well, for as a
hogge in his life time is alwayes deuouring, and neuer commo-
dious in aught till his death, euen ſo is he whoſe goods at that
time may be put to many good vſes.
   Had. And ſo I hope they ſhall before his death, this daughter of his, did, and I thinke doth loueme, but I then thinking my 80
ſelfe worthy of an Empreſſe, gaue but ſlight reſpect vnto her
fauour, for that her parentage ſem'd not to equall my high
thoughts, puft vp,
   Li, With Tobacco ſurely,
   Had No but with as bad a weede, vaineglory.
   Li. And you could now be content, to put your lofty ſpirits
into the loweſt pit of her fauour: VVhy what meanes will ſerue
man, Sfoote if all I haue will repaire thy fortunes, it ſhall fly at
thy commaund,
   Ha. Thankes good Coze, the meanes ſhall not be great, on- 90
ly that I may firſt be clad in a generous outſide, for that is the
chiefe attraction, that drawes female affection; good parts
without any abilements of gallantry, are no more ſet by in
theſe times, then a good legge in a wollen ſtocken: No, tis
a gliſtering preſence and audacity brings women into fooles
felicity.

B 2

Li

Li. Yaue a good confidence Coze, but what deendien your braue outſide ſhall effect.

Had. That being had wele to the Vſurer where you ſhal of-fer ſome ſlight peece of land to mortgage, and if you doe it to bring our ſelues into caſh, it ſhall be nere the farther from you, for heres a proiect will not be fruſtrate of this purpoſe.

Li. That ſhal be ſhortly tryed, Ile inſtantly go ſeeke for a habit for thee and that of the richeſt too, that which ſhall not be ſubiect to the ſcoffe of any gallant, though to the accompli-ſhing thereof all my meanes goes: Alas whats a man vnleſſe he weare good cloathes.   *Exit Lightfoote*

Had. Good ſpeed attend my ſuite, heres a neuer ſeene Ne-phewe kind in diſtreſſe, this giues me more cauſe of admiration then the loſſe of xxxv. ſettings together at Paſſage. I when tis performed, but wordsand deeds are now more different then Puritans and Players.   *Enter Atlas*

At. Heres the Player would ſpeake with you.

Had. About the Iigge, I promis’d him, my penne and inke, I prethee let him in, there may be ſome Caſh rim’d out of him.
          Enter Player.

Pla. The Muſes afsiſt you ſir, what at your ſtudy ſo early.

Ha O chiefely now ſir for (*aurora muſis amicat*)

Pla. Indeed I vnderſtand not latine ſir.

Ha. You muſt then pardon me, good M. Chaunge-coate, for I proteſt vntee it is ſo much my often conuerſe, that if there be none but women in my company, yet cannot I forbeare it.

Pla. That ſhewes your more learning ſir, but I pray you is that ſmall matter done I intreated for.

Ha. A ſmall matter, youle finde it worth *Megge* of Weſt-minſter, althouh it be but a bare Iigge.

Pla. O lord ſir, I would it had but halfe the taſte of garlicke.

Ha. Garlicke ſtinkes to this, proue that you haue not more whores to ſee this, then ere Garlicke had, ſay I am a boaſter of mine owne workes, diſgrace me on the open ſtage, and bob me off with nere a penny.

Pla. O lord ſir, farre be it from vs, to debarre any worthy writer of his merit; but I pray you ſir, what is the title you be-ſtow vpon it?

                                        Ha. Ma-

Ha. Marry that which is full as forceable as Garlicke, the name of it is *Who buyes my fowre ropes of hard Onions*, by which fowre ropes is meant fowre ſeuerall kind of liuers, by the onions hangers on, as at ſome conuenient time I wil more par-ticularly informe you in ſo rare a hidden and obſcure a miſtery.

Pla. I pray let me ſee the beginning of it, I hope you haue made no dark ſentence in't, for Ile aſſure you our audience cõmõly are very ſimple idle-headed people, & if they ſhould heare what they vnderſtand not, they would quite forſake our houſe.

Ha. O nere feare it, for what I haue writ is both witty to the wiſe, and pleaſing to the ignorant; for you ſhall haue theſe laugh at it farre more heartily that vnderſtand it not, then thoſe that doe.

Pla. Me thinke the end of this ſtaffe is a foote too long.

Ha. O no, ſing it but in tune, and I dare warrant you.

Pla, Why heare ye,   *He ſings*
    And you that delight in truls and minions,
    Come buy my fowre ropes of hard S. Thomas onions:
Looke you there S. Thomas might very wel haue been left out, beſides, hard ſhould haue eome next the onions,

Ha. Fie no, the diſmembring of a rime to bring in reaſon ſhcwes the more efficacy in the writer.

Pla. Well as you pleaſe, I pray you ſir what wil the gratuity be, I would content you as neere hand as I could.

Ha. So I beleeue,   *aſide*;
Why M. Change-coate, I do not ſuppoſe we ſhall differ many pounds, pray make your offer, if you giue me too much, I will moſt Doctor of Phiſicke like reſtoare.

Pla. You ſay well, looke you ſir, theres a brace of angels, beſides much drinke of free coſt if it be lik't.

Ha. How M. Change-coate a brace of angels beſides much drinke of free coſt if it be lik't, I feare you haue learned it by heart, if you haue powdred vp my plot in your ſconce, you may home ſir and inſtruct your Poet ouer a pot of ale, the whole me-thode on't, but if you do ſo iuggle, looke too't Shrouetuſeday is at hand, and I haue ſome acquaintance with Bricklayers and Playſterers.

Pla. Nay, I pray ſir be not angry, for as I am a true ſtage-

trotter

trotter, I meane honeſtly and looke ye, more for your loue then otherwiſe, I giue you a brace more.

Had. Well, good words doe much, I cannot now be angry with you, but ſee henceforward, you doe like him that would pleaſe a new married wife, ſhew your moſt at firſt, leaſt ſome other come betweene you and your deſires, for I proteſt had you not ſuddenly ſhowne your good nature, another ſhould haue had it though t'ad bin for nothing.

Pla. Troth I am ſory I gaue you ſuch cauſe of impatiency, but you ſhall ſee hereafter if your inuention take, I will not ſtand off for a brace more or leſſe, deſiring I may ſee your works before another.

Ha. Nay before al others, and ſhotly expect a notable peece of matter ſuch a Iigge whoſe tune with the naturall whiſtle of a carman, ſhall be more rauiſhing to the eares of ſhopkeepers then a whole conſort of barbors at midnight.

Pla. I am your man for't, I pray you commaund al the kindneſſe belongs to my function, as a box for your friend at a new play although I procure the hate of all my company.

Had. No Ile pay for it rather, that may breede a muteny in your whole houſe.

Pla. I care not, I ha plaid a Kings part anie time theſe ten yeeres, if I cannot commaund ſuch a matter twere poore ifaith.

Ha. Well Maiſter chaungecoate you ſhal now leaue me, for Ile to my ſtudie, the morning houres are precious and my muſe meditates moſt vpon an empty ſtomacke.

Pla. I pray ſir when this new inuention is produc't let not me be forgotten.

Ha. Ile ſooner forget to be a Iigge maker.

Exit plaier.

So heres foure angels I little dreampt of. Nay and there bee mony to be gotten by foolery, I hope fortune will not ſee me want. *Atlas, Atlas.*   (*Enter Atlas.*

What was my country coſe here ſince.

At. Why did he promiſe to come againe ſeeing how the caſe ſtoode wye.

Ha. Ye and to aduaunce my downe falne fortunes Atlas.

At. But ye are not ſure a meant it yee when he ſpake it.

Ha. No

Ha. No nor is it in man to coniecture rightly the thought by the tongue.

At. Why then ile beleeue it when I ſee it, if you had beene in proſperitie when a had promiſty ou this kindeneſſe,

Ha. I had not needed it.

At. But being now you doe, I feare you mnſt goe without it.

Ha. If I doe *Atlas* be it ſo, ile ene goe write this rime ouer my beds head.

Vndone by folly, fortune lend me more,

Canſt thou, and wilt not, pox on ſuch a whore,   220

And ſo ile ſet vp my reſt, but ſee *Atlas* heres a little of that that dambs Lawyers, take it in part of a further recompence.

Atlas No pray keepe it, I am conceited of your better fortunes, and therefore will ſtay out that expectation.

Ha. Why if you will you may, but the ſurmounting of my fortunes is as much to be doubted, as he whoſe eſtate lies in the lotterie, deſperate.

At. But nere deſpaire ſfoote why ſhould not you liue aſwel as a thouſand others, that were change of taffety, whoſe meanes were neuer any thing.   230

Ha. Yes cheating, theft, and pandariſing, or may be flattery, I haue maintained ſome of them my ſelfe, but come haſt aught to breakefaſt.

At. Yes theres the fagg end of a leg of mutton,

Ha. There cãnot be a ſweeter diſh, it has Coſt mony the dreſ-

At. At the barbours you meane.   *Exeunt.*   (ſing.

Enter Albert ſolus.   I.ii.

At. This is the greene, and this the chamberwindow, and ſee appointed light ſtands in the caſement, the ladder of ropes ſet orderly, yet he that ſhould aſcend, ſlow in his haſt, is not as yet 240 come hether.

Wert any friend that liues but *Carracus*

I'de trie the bliſſe which this fine time preſents.

Appoint to carry hence ſo rare an heire,

And be ſo ſlacke ſfoote a doth moue my patience,

Would any man that is not voide of ſence

Not haue watcht night by night for ſuch a priſe,

Her beauties ſo attractiue, that by heauen,

My

My heart halfe graunts to doe my friend a wrong,
250 Forgoe thefe thoughts for *Albert* be not flaue
To thy affection doe not falfifie
Thy faith to him, whofe onely friendfhips worth
A world of women, hee is fuch a one,
Thou canft not liue without his good.
A is and was euer, as thine owne harts blood,
Sfoot fee fhee beckens me for *Carracus*,   *Maria beckens him*
Shall my bafe purity, caufe me neglect,   *in the window.*
This prefent happineffe, I will obteyne it,
Spight of my tymerous Confcience, I am in perfon,
260 Habit and all fo like to *Carracus*,
It may be acted, and neere called in queftion.
    Ma. cals Hift *Carracus* afcend.
All is as cleere as in our hearts we wifht.
    Alb. Nay, if I goe not now, I might be gelded ifaith.
        Albert *afcends, and being on the top of the ladder,*
                    puts outs the candle.
    Ma. O loue, why doe you foe.
    Alb. I heard the fteps of fome comming this way,
Did you not heare *Albert* paffe by as yet.
270   *Ma.* Nor any Creature paffe this way this howre.
    Alb. Then hee intends iuft at the breake of day,
To lend his trufty helpe to our departure:
Tis yet two howres time thither, till when lets reft,
For that our fpeedy flight, will not yeeld any.
    Ma. But I feare we poffeffing of each others prefence,
fhall ouerflip the time, will your friend call.
    Alb. Iuft at the inftant, feare not of his Care:
    Ma. Come then deere *Carracus*, thou now fhalt reft,
Vpon that bed, where fancy oft hath thought thee;
280 Which kindneffe vntill now, I nere did graunt thee,
Nor would I now, but that thy loyall faith
I haue fo often tride, euen now,
Seeing thee come to that moft honored end,
Through all the dangers, which blacke night prefents,
For to conuey me hence and marry me.
    Alb. If I doe not doe fo, then hate me euer,

                                                        Ma.

Ma. I doe beleeue thee, and will hate thee neuer. *Exeunt.*
Enter Carracus.

How pleaſing are the ſteps we louers make,
When in the paths of our content wee pace,
To meet our longings: what happineſſe it is
Man to loue. But oh, what greater bliſſe
To loue, and be beloued: O what one vertue,
Ere raignd in me, that I ſhould be inricht,
With all Earths good at once, I haue a friend,
Selected by the heauens, as a gift,
To make me happy, whilſt I liue one earth,
A man ſo rare of goodneſſe, firme of faith,
That Earths Content muſt vaniſh in his death.
Then for my loue, and miſtris of my ſoule,
A maid of rich endowments, beautified
With all the vertues nature could beſtow
Vpon mortality, who this happy night
Will make me gainer of her heauenly ſelfe,
And ſee how ſuddenly I haue attaind,
To the abode of my deſired wiſhes;
This is the greene, how darke the night appeares,
Icannot heare the tread of my true friend,
Albert, hiſt *Albert*, hees not come as yet,
Nor is thappointed light ſet in the window.
What if I call? *Maria*, it may be
Shee feard to ſet a light, and onely harkeneth
To heare my ſteps, and yet I dare not call,
Leaſt I betray my ſelfe, and that my voice,
Thinking to enter in the eares of her,
Be of ſome other heard: no I will ſtay
Vntill the comming of my deare friend *Albert*.
But now thinke *Carracus*, what the end will be
Of this thou doſt determine, thou art come
Hether to Rob a father of that wealth,
That ſoly lengthens his now drooping yeares,
His vertuous daughter, and all of that ſex left,
To make him happy in his aged dayes,
The loſſe of her, may cauſe him to diſpaire,

C

Tranſ-

Tranſport his nere decaying ſence to frenzie,
Or to ſome ſuch abhorred inconuenience,
Whereto fraile age is ſubiect, I do too il in this,
And muſt not thinke but that a fathers plaint,
Wil moue the Heauens, to power forth miſery,
330 Vpon the head of diſobediency,
Yet reaſon tels vs, parents are oreſeene,
VVhen with two ſtrictt a reine they do hold in,
Their childs affections, and controule that loue,
VVhich the high powers deuine inſpires them with,
VVhen in their ſhalloweſt iudgements they may know
Affection croſt, brings miſery and woe:
But whilſt I run contemplating on this,
I ſoftly pace to my deſired bliſſe,
Ile goe into the next field, where my friend,
340 Told me the horſes were in readineſſe.   *Exit.*
I. iv.   *Albert deſcending from Maria,*
   Ma. But do not ſtay, what if you finde not *Albert,*
   Alb, Ile then retourne alone to fetch you hence,
   Ma. If you ſhould now deceaue me, hauing gain'd, what you
men ſeeke for.
   Alb. Sooner ile deceaue my ſoule, and ſo I feare I haue.
   Ma. At your firſt call I will deſcend.
   Alb. Till when, this touch of lips be the true pleadge,
of *Carracus* conſtant true deuoted loue,
350   *Ma.* Be ſure you ſtay not long, farewell,
I cannot lend an eare to heare you part,   *Exit Ma.*
   Alb. But you did lend a hand vnto my entrance. *He deſcends*
How haue I wrong'd my friend, my faithfull friend,
Robd him of whats more precious then his blood,
His earthly heauen th'unſpotted honor,
Of his ſoule-ioying Miſtres, the fruition of whoſe bed,
I yet am warme of, whilſt deere *Carracus,*
Wanders this cold night, through th'unſheltering field,
Seeking me treacherous man, yet no man neither,
360 Though in an outward ſhew of ſuch appearance,
But am a Diuel indeed, for ſo this deed,
Of wronged loue and friendſhip rightly makes me,

                                             I may

I may compare my friend, to one that's ſicke,
Who lying on his death-bed, cals to him,
His dear'ſt thought friend and bids him goe,
To ſome rare gifted man that can reſtore,
His former health, this his friend ſadly heares,
And vowes with proteſtations to fulfill,
His wiſht deſires, with his beſt performance,
But then no ſooner ſeeing that the death,   370
Of his ſicke friend, would ad to him ſome gaine.
Goes not to ſeeke a remedy to ſaue,
But like a wretch hides him to dig his graue,
As I haue done for vertuous *Carracus*,
Yet *Albert* be not reaſonleſſe, to indanger,
VVhat thou maiſt yet ſecure, who can deteƈt,
The crime of thy licentious appetite,
I here ones pace tis ſurely *Carracus*.   *Enter Carracus.*
    Ca. Not finde my friend, ſure ſome malignant plannet,
Rules ore this night, and enuying the content,   380
VVhich I in thought poſſeſſe, debarres me thus,
From what is more then happy, the loued preſence of a deare
friend and loue,
    Alb. Tis wronged *Carracus* by *Alberts* baſeneſſe,
I haue no power now to reueale my ſelfe,
    Car. The horſes ſtand at the appointed place,
And nights darke couerture, makes firme our ſafety,
My friend is ſurely falne into a ſlumber,
On ſome bancke hereabouts, I will call him,
Friend, *Albert*, *Albert*.   390
    Alb What ere you are that call, you know my name.
    Ca. I, and thy heart deare friend:
    Alb. O *Carracus*, you are a ſlow pac't louer.
Your credit had been toucht, had I not beene:
    Ca. As how I preethee *Albert*:
    Alb Why I excuſd you to the faire *Maria*;
Who would haue thought you elſe, a ſlacke performer.
For comming firſt vnder her chamber window,
Shee heard me tread, and cald vpon your name,
To which I anſwered with a tongue like yours: 400

C 2

And

And told her, I would goe to ſeeke for *Albert*,
And ſtraight retourne.
    Ca. Whom I haue found, thankes to thy faith, and heauen.
But had not ſhee a light, when you came firſt?
    Alb. Yes but hearing of ſome Company,
Shee at my warning, was forc't to put it out:
And had I bin ſo too, you and I too had ſtill bin happy.   *aſide*
    Ca. See we are now come to the chamber window.
    Al. Then you muſt call, for ſo I ſaid I would,
410   *Ca. Maria.*
    Ma. My *Carracus*, are you ſo ſoone retournd?
I ſee, youle keepe your promiſe.
    Ca. VVho would not doe ſo, hauing paſt it thee,
Cannot be framd of aught but trechery:
Faireſt deſcend, that by our hence departing,
VVe may make firme the bliſſe of our content.
    Ma. Is your friend *Albert* with you?
    Alb. Yes, and your ſeruant honored Lady.
    Ma. Hold me from falling *Carracus.*   *ſhee deſcends.*
420   *Ca.* I will do now ſo; but not at other times.
    Ma, You are merry ſir:
But what d'ee intend with this your ſcaling ladder,
To leaue it thus, or put it forth of ſight?
    Ca. Faithts no great matter which:
Yet we will take it hence, that it may breed
Many confuſd opinions in the houſe
Of your eſcape here: *Albert* you ſhall beare it:
It may bee you may chaunce to practiſe that way;
VVhich when you do, may your attempts ſo proue
430 As mine haue done, moſt fortunate in loue.
    Alb. May you continew euer ſo:
But its time now to make ſome haſt to horſe:
Night ſoone will vaniſh: O that it had power
For euer to exclude day from oureies,
For my lookes then will ſhew my villany: *aſide*
    Car. Come faire *Maria* the troubles of this night,
Are as forerunners to enſuing pleaſures,
And noble friend although now *Carracus*

Seemes

Seemes in the gaining of this beautious priſe.
To keepe from you ſo muchof his lou'd treaſure,   440
Which ought not be mixted, yet his heart
Shall ſo farre ſtriue in your wiſh't happineſſe,
That if the loſſe and ruine of it ſelfe can but auaile your good
  Alb. O friend, no more, come, you are ſlow in haſte,
Friendſhip ought neuer be diſtruſt in words,
Till all her deeds be finiſh't, who looking in a booke,
And reades but ſome part only, cannot iudge
What prayſe the whole deſerues, becauſe his knowledge
Is grounded but on part, as thine friend is   *aſide,*
Ignorant of that black miſchiefe I haue done thee.   450
  Ma. Carracus I am weary, are the horſes farre?
  Ca. No faireſt, we are now euen at them:
Come, do you follow *Albert?*
  Alb. Yes I do follow, would I had done ſo euer,
And nere had gone before.   *Exeunt.*

Actus Secundus. II.i.

Enter Hogge *the Uſurer, with* Peter *ſeruitude truſsing his points.*
  Ho. What hath not my young lord *Wealthy* been here this
morning?
  Pe. No in very deed ſir, is a towardly young gentleman,   460
ſhall a haue my young Miſtris, your daughter, I pray youſir?
  Ho. I that a ſhall *Peter,* ſhe cannot be matched to greater
honour and riches in all this Country; yet the peeuiſh girle
makes coy of it, ſhe had rather affect a Prodigall, as there was
Hadit, one that by this time cannot be otherwiſe then hang'd,
or in ſome worſe eſtate, yet ſhee would haue had him, but I
prayſe my ſtarres ſhee went without him though, I did not
without's lands 'twas a rare mortgage *Peter?*
  Pe. As ere came in parchment, but ſee, here comes my young
lord.   *Enter young L. Wealthy.*   470
  We. Morrow father *Hogge,* I come to tel you ſtrange newes,
my ſiſter is ſtolne away to night, tis thought by Nigromancy,
what Nigromancy is, I leaue to the readers of the ſeauen cham-
pions of chiſtendome.

C 3

Ho.

Ho. But is it poſsible your ſiſter ſhould be ſtolne, ſure ſome of the houſhold ſeruants were confederates in't.

Wel. Faith, I thinke they would haue confeſt then, for I am ſure my lord and father hath put them all to the baſtinado twice this morning already, not a wayting-woman but has been ſtowed ifaith.

Pe. Truſt me a ſayes wel for the moſt part.

Ho. Then my lord your father is farre impatient.

We. Impatient, I ha ſeene the picture of *Hector* in a Haberdaſhers ſhop, not looke halfe ſo furious, he appeares more terrible then wilde fire at a play. But father *Hogge*, when is the time your daughter and I ſhall to this wedlock druggery.

Ho. Troth my lord when you pleaſe, ſhee's at your diſpoſure, and I reſt much thankfull that your Lordſhip will ſo highly honour me, ſhe ſhal haue a good portion my lord, though nothing in reſpect of your large reuenues; call her in *Peter*, tel her my moſt reſpected lord *Welthies* here, to whoſe preſence I will now commit her, and I pray you my Lord, proſecute the gaine of her affectation with the beſt affecting words you may, and ſo I bid good morrow to your lordſhip   *Exit Ho.*

We. Moreouer, father *Hogge*, to proſecute the gaine of her affectation with the beſt affecting words, as I am a Lord, a moſt rare phraſe: well I perceiue age is not altogether ignorant, though many an old Iuſtice is ſo.   *Enter Peter.*
How now *Peter* is thy young miſtris vp yet?

Pe. Yes indeed ſhee's an early ſtirrer, and I doubt not hereafter, but that your lordſhip may ſay ſhee's abroad before you can riſe.

We. Faith and ſo ſhe may, for tis long ere I can get vp when I goe foxt to bed; but *Peter* has ſhe no other ſuters beſides my ſelfe.

Pe. No and it like your lordſhip, nor is fit ſhe ſhould.

We. Not fit ſhe ſhould, I tell thee *Peter*, I would giue away as much as ſome Knights are worth, and that's not much, only to wipe the noſes of ſome dozen or two of Gallants, and to ſee how pittifully thoſe percels of mans fleſh would looke when I had caught the bird, which they had beaten the buſh for.

Pe. Indeed your lordſhips conqueſt would haue ſeem'd the greater.   *We.*

We. Foot, as I am a Lo. it angers me to the guts, that no bo-
dy hath been about her.

Pe. For any thing I know, your lordſhip may goe without
her.

We. An I could haue inioin'd her to ſome pale fac't louers
diſtraction, or beene enuied for my happineſſe, it had beene
ſomewhat.   520

Enter Rebecka Hogs daughter.

But ſee where ſhee comes, I knewe ſhe had not power enough
to ſtay another ſending, for ô lords! what are we? our very
names enforce beauty to fly, being ſent for aſide.
Morrow pretty Becke: how dooſt?

Re. I rather ſhould enquire your lordſhips health, ſeeing
you vp at ſuch an early hower: was it the tooth-ake, or elſe
fleas diſturb'd you?

We. Dee ye think I am ſubiect to ſuch common infirmities?
nay, were I diſeas'd I'de ſcorne but to be diſeas'd like a lord   530
ifaith: but I can tell you newes, your fellow virgin-hole player, my ſiſter is ſtolne away to night.

Re. Intruth I am glad on't ſhee's now free from the iealous
eye of a father; do not yee ſuſpect, my lord, who it ſhould be
that hath carried her away?

We. No, nor care not, as ſhe brewes, ſo let her bake, ſo ſayd
the auntient prouerbe, but lady mine that ſhalbe, your father
hath wiſht me to appoint the day with you.

Re. What day my lord?

We. Why of mariage, as the learned Hiſtoriographer writes   540
hymens hollidaies, or nuptial Ceremonious rites.

Re. Why, when would you appoint that my lord?

We. Why let me ſee, I thinke the Taylor may diſpatch all
our veſtures in a weeke: therefore, it ſhall be directly this day
ſennight.

Pe. God giue you ioy.

Re. Of what I pray you impudence, this fellow wil go neere
to take his oath that he hath ſeene vs plighted faiths together,
my father keeps him for no other cauſe, then to outſweare the
truth. My lord not to hold you any longer in a fooles paradice,   550
nor to blind you with the hopes I neuer intend to accompliſh,
know

know I neither doe, can, or will loue you.

We. How, not loue a lord; ô indiſcreete young woman! Indeed your father told me how vnripe I ſhould finde you: but al's, one vnripe fruit will aske more ſhaking before they fall, then thoſe that are, and my conqueſt will ſeeme the greater ſtill.

Pe. Afore god is a moſt vnanſwerable lord, and holds her toot ifaith.

560 *We.* Nay ye could not a pleas'd me better, then ſeeing you ſo inuincible, and ſuch a difficult attaining to, I would not giue a pin for the ſociety of a female that ſhould ſeeme willing, but giue me a wench that hath diſdainefull lookes:
For tis denial whets on appetite,
When proferred ſeruice doth allay delight.

Re. The fooles well read in vice, my lord, I hope you here-after will no further inſinuate in the courſe of your affections, and for the better withdrawing from them, you may pleaſe to know, I haue irreuocably decreed neuer to marry.

570 *We.* Neuer to marry, *Peter*, I pray beare witnes of her words that when I haue attain'd her, it may adde to my fame and con-queſt.

Pe. Yes indeed an't like your lordſhip.

We. Nay, ye muſt think *Becke* I know how to woe, ye ſhall finde no baſhfull vniuerſity man of me,

Re. Indeed I thinke y'ad nere that bringing vp, did you e-uer ſtudy my lord?

We. Yes faith that I haue, and the laſt week too, three dayes and a night together.

580 *Re.* About what I pray?

We. Onely to finde out, why a woman going on the right ſide of her husband the day time, ſhould lie on his left ſide at night; and as I am a lord, I neuer knew the meaning on't till yeſterday, Mallapert my fathers Butler being a witty Iacka-napes told me why it was.

Re. Berlady, my lord, twas a ſhrewd ſtuddy, and I feare hath altered the property of your good parts, for ile aſſure you I lou'd you a fortnight a goe farre better.

We. Nay, tis all one whether you doe or no, tis but a little

more

more trouble to bring ye about agen, & no queſtion but a man 590
may doot; I am he, tis true as your father ſayd, the blacke Oxe
hath not trode vpon that foote of yours.

    Re. No, but the white Calfe hath, and ſo I leaue your lord-
ſhip.   *Exit Re.*

    We. Wel go thy waies, th'art as witty a marmaled eater, as
euer I conuerſt with; now, as I am a lord, I loue her better and
better, ile home and Poetiſe vpon her good parts preſently, *Peter* heres apreparatiue to my further applications, and *Peter*
be circumſpect in giuing me diligent notice, what ſutors ſeeme
to be pee-ping.   600

    Pe. Ile warrant you my lord, ſhee's your owne, for ile giue
out to all that comes neere her, that ſhees betrothed to you, and
if the worſt come to the worſt, Ile ſweare it.

    We. Why god-a-mercy, and if euer I do gaine my requeſt,
Thou ſhalt in brauer cloathes be ſhortly dreſt.   *Exeunt.*

            Enter old L. Wealthy ſolus.   II.ii.
Haue the fates then conſpir'd, and quite bereft
My drooping yeeres, of all the bleſt content
That age partakes of, by the ſweet aſpect
Of their well nurtur'd iſſue; whoſe obedience,   610
Diſcreete and duteous haueour, onely lengthens
The thred of age; when on the contrary,
By rude demeanour and their headſtrong wils,
That thred's ſoone rauel'd out: O why *Maria*
Couldſt thou abandon me now at this time,
When my gray head's declining to the graue!
Could any Maſculine flatterer on earth
So far bewitch thee, to forget thy ſelfe,
As now to leaue me? Did Nature ſoly giue thee me,
As my chiefe ineſtimable treaſure,   620
Whereby my age might paſſe in quiet to reſt:
And art thou prov'd to be the only curſe,
Which heauen could throw vpon mortality:
Yet ile not curſe thee, though I feare the fates
Will on thy head inflict ſome puniſhment,
Which I will daily pray they may with-hold;
                D   Al-

Although thy disobediency deserues
Extreamest rigor, yet I wish to thee
Content in loue full of tranquility.   *Enter young Welthy.*
630 But see where stands my shame, whose indiscretion
Doth seeme to bury all the liuing honours,
Of all our auncestours but tis the fates decree,
That men might know their weake mortality.
   We. Sir, I cannot finde my sister,
   Fa. I know thou canst not, t'were to rare to see
VVisdome found out by ignorance.
   We. How father, is it not possible that wisdome should be
found out by ignorance; I pray then how do many Magnificoes
come by it?
640   *Fa.* Not buy it sonne, as you had need to doe,
Yet wealth without that, may liue more content,
Then wits enioyers, can debard of wealth,
All pray for wealth, but I nere hard yet,
Of anie but one, that ere praid for wit,
Hees counted wise enough in these vaine times,
That hath but meanes enough to weare gay clothes,
And be an outside of humanitie; what matters it a pin,
How indiscreet so ere a naturall be,
So that his wealth be great, thats it doth cause
650 VVisdome in these daies; to giue fooles applause,
And when gay folly speakes, how vaine so ere,
VVisdome must silent sit, and speech forbeare.
   We. Then wisdome will sit as mute as learning among many
Courtiers, but father I partlie suspect that *Carracus* hath got
my sister.
   Fa. With Childe, I feare ere this.
   We. Berlady and that may be true, but whether a has or no,
its al one, if you please, Ile take her from vnder his nose in spight
ons teeth, and aske him no leaue.
660   *Fa.* That were to headstrong, sonne, weele rather leaue them
to the will of heauen.
To fall or prosper, and though young *Carracus*
Be but a gentleman of small reuennews;
Yet he deserues my daughter for his vertues,

And

And had I though ſhee could not be withdrawne
From th'affecting of him, I had ere this
Made them both happy by my free conſent
VVhich now I wiſh I had graunted, and ſtill pray
If any haue her, it may be *Carracus*.

   We. Troth and I wiſh ſo too, for in my minde hees a gent. of 670
a good houſe, and ſpeakes true lattine,

   Fa. To morrow ſonne, you ſhall ride to his houſe
And there enquier of your ſiſters being,
But as you tender me, and your owne good
Vſe no rough language ſauouring of diſtaſt,
Or any vnciuil tearmes.

   We. Why doe ye take me for a mid-wife,

   Fa. But tell young *Carracus* theſe words from me,
That if he hath with ſafegard of her honor,
Eſpouſd my daughter, that I then forgiue 680
His raſh offence, and will accept of him,
In all the fatherly loue, I owe a childe.

   We. I am ſure my ſiſter willbe glad to heare it, and I cannot
blame her, for ſheele then inioy that with quietneſſe, which many a wench in theſe dayes doesſcratch for,

   Fa. Come ſonne, ile wright to *Carracus*, that my owne
hand may witneſſe, how much I ſtand affected to his worth.

                                            Exeunt.

     Enter Haddid in his gay apparel, making him ready, and   II.iii.
               with him Lightfoote.   690

   Had. By this light Coze, this ſuite does rarely: the taylor
that made it, may happe to be ſaued, ant be but for his good
workes, I thinke I ſhall be proud of em, and ſo I was neuer yet
of any clothes.

   Li. How not of your Clothes, why then you were neuer
proud of any thing, for therein chiefly conſiſteth pride: for you
neuer ſaw pride pictured, but in gay attire.

   Ha. True, but in my opinion, pride might as well be por-
traied in any other ſhape, as to ſeeme to be an affector of gallantry, being the cauſes thereof are ſo ſeuerall and diuers, as 700
ſome are proud of their ſtrength, although that pride coſt them
the loſſe of a limbe or two, by ouer-daring, likewiſe ſome are

                          D 2   proud

proud of their humor, although in that humor, they be often
knockt for being ſo, ſome are proud of their drinke, although
that liquid operation, cauſe them to weare a night-cap 3. weeks
after, ſome are proud of their good parts, although they neuer
put them to better vſes, then the enioying of a common ſtrum-
pets company, and are only made proud by the fauor of a wai-
ting woman, others are proud———

710 *Li.* Nay, I preethee Coze, enough of pride, but when do you
entend to go yonder to Couetouſneſſe the Vſurer, that we may
ſee how neere your plot wil take, for the releaſing of your mortgag'd lands.

 Ha. Why now preſently, and if I do not accompliſh my pro-
iects to a wiſhed end, I wiſh my fortunes may be like ſome ſcra-
ping tradeſman, that neuer embraceth true pleaſure, till he be
threeſcore and ten.

 Li. But ſay *Hogs* daughter, on whom all your hopes depend
by this be betrothed to ſome other.

720 *Ha.* VVhy ſay ſhee were, nay more, maried to another, I
would be neare the further of them effecting of my intents, no
Coze, I partly know her inward diſpoſition, and did I but only
know her to be woman kind, I thinke it were ſufficient.

 Li. Sufficient, for what.

 Had. VVhy to obtaine a graunt of the beſt thing ſhee had,
Chaſtity, Man tis not here, as tis with you in the Countrey, not
to be had without fathers and mothers good will, no, the City
is a place of more traffique, where each one learnes by example
of their elders, to make the moſt of their owne, either for profit
730 or pleaſure.

 Li. Tis but your miſbeleeuing thoughts, makes you ſurmiſe
ſo, if women were ſo kind, how haps you had not by their fa-
uors kept your ſelfe out of the clawes of pouerty.

 Had. O but Coze, Can a ſhip ſaile without water, had I had
but ſuch a ſuite as this, to ſet my ſelfe a floate, I would not haue
fear'd ſincking, but come, no more of need, now to the Vſurer,
andthough all hopes do faile, a man can want no liuing, So long
as ſweet deſire reignes in women.

 Li. But then your ſelfe muſt able be in giuing.

740   *Exeunt.*

Ente

Enter Albert folus.　　　　　　　　　　　　　II.iv.

Confcience thou horror vnto wicked men,
VVhen wilt thou ceafe thy all afflicted wrath,
And fet my foule free from the laborinth
Of thy tormenting terror; O but it fits not,
Should I defire redreffe or wifh for comfort,
That haue committed an act fo inhumane,
Able to fill fhames fpatious Chronicle.
Who but a damn'd one, could haue done like me,
Robd my deere friend, in a fhort moments time　　　750
Of his loues high pri'zd Iem of Chaftity:
That which fo many yeeres himfelfe hath ftaid for;
How often hath he as he lay in bed,
Sweetly difcourft to me of his *Maria?*
And with what pleafiing paffions a did fuffer
Loues genle war-fiege, then he would relate
How he firft came vnto her faire eyes view;
How long it was ere fhee could brooke affection,
And then how conftant fhee did ftill abide:
I then at this would ioy, as if my breft　　　　760
Had fimpathi'zd in equall happineffe;
With my true friend: but now when ioy fhould be,
VVho but a damn'd one would haue done like me:
He hath been married now at leaft a moneth:
In all which time I haue not once beheld him; This is his houfe:
Ile call to know his health, but will not fee him,
My lookes would then betray me, for fhould he afke
My caufe of feeming fadneffe, or the like;
I could not but reueale, and fo pourd on
VVorfe vnto ill, which breeds confufion.　　　　770

　　　He knocks, Enter Seruingman.
Ser. To what intent dee knocke fir.
Al. Becaufe I wold be heard fir, is the M^r. of this houfe within?
Ser. Yes marry is a fir, would you fpeake with him?
Alb. My bufineffe is not fo troublefome:
Is a in health with his late efpoufed wife.
Ser. Both are exceeding well fir.
Alb. Ime truly glad ont, farewel good friend.

D 3

Ser. I

  Ser. I pray you lets craue your name ſir, I may els haue anger.
780 *Alb.* You may ſay, one *Albert* riding by this way, onely
inquir'd their health.
  Ser. I will acquaint ſo much.   *Exit Ser.*
  Alb. How like a poiſonous Doctor haue I come,
To enquire their wel-fare, knowing that my ſelfe
Haue giuen the portion of their nere recouery;
For which I will afflict my ſelfe with torture euer:
And ſince the earth yeelds not a remedy,
Able to ſalue the ſores my luſt hath made,
Ile now take fare-wel of ſociety,
790 And th'aboade of men to entertaine a life
Fitting my fellowſhip, in deſart woods;
Where beaſts like me conſort, there may I liue,
Farre off from wronging vertuous *Carracus*;
Theres no *Maria* that ſhall ſatisfie
My hatefull luſt, the trees ſhall ſhelter
This wretched trunke of mine, vpon whoſe backe,
I will engraue the ſtory of my ſinne,
And there this ſhort breath of mortality,
Ile finiſh vp in that repentant ſtate;
800 Where not th'allurements of earths vanities
Can ere ore-take me, there's no baites for luſt,
No friend to ruine, I ſhall then be free
From practiſing the art of treachery;
Thither then ſteps where ſuch content abides,
Where penitency not diſturb'd may greeue,
Where on each tree and ſpringing plant, Ile carue
This heauy motto of my miſery.
Who but a damb'd one could haue done like me?
Carracus farewel, if ere thou ſeeſt me more,
810 Shalt finde me curing of a ſole-ſicke ſore. *Exit.*

III.i.   # Actus Tertius.

   Enter Carracus *driuing his man before him.*
  Ca. Why thou baſe villaine, was my deareſt friend here, and
couldſt not make him ſtay?

                 Ser.

Ser. Sfoote ſir, I could not force him againſt his wil, an a
had been a woman.

Ca. Hence thou vntuter'd ſlaue.   *Exit Ser.*
But couldſt thou *Albert* come ſo nere my dore, and not vouch-
ſafe the comfort of thy preſence?
Hath my good fortune caus'd thee to repine?   820
And ſeeing my ſtate ſo full repleate with good,
Canſt thou with-draw thy loue to leſſen it?
What could ſo moue thee, was't becauſe I married?
Didſt thou imagine I infring'd my faith,
For that a woman did participate
In equall ſhare with thee? Cannot my friendſhip
Be firme to thee, becauſe tis deare to her;
Yet no more deere to her then firme to thee:
Beleeue me *Albert*, thou doſt little thinke,
How much thy abſence giues cauſe of diſcontent,   830
But ile impute it onely to neglect,
It is neglect indeed when friends neglect
The ſight of friends, and ſay tis troubleſome;
Onely aske how they do, and ſo farewell:
Shewing an outward kinde of ſeeming duty,
Which in the rules of manhood is obſeru'd
And thinke full well they haue performd their taske,
When of their friends health they do onely aske,
Not caring how they are, or how diſtreſt,
It is enough they haue their loues expreſt,   840
In bare enquiry, and in theſe times too
Friendſhips ſo cold that fewe ſo much will doe:
And am not I beholding then to *Albert*,
He after knowlede of our being well,
Sayd he was truly glad on't: ô rare friend!
If he be vnkind how many more may mend;
But whether am I carried by vnkindneſſe?
Why ſhould not I as wel ſet light by friendſhip,
Since I haue ſeene a man whom I late thought,
Had been compos'd of nothing but of faith,   850
Proue ſo regardleſſe of his friends content.   *Enter Maria*

Ma. Come *Carracus* I haue ſought you all about,
Your ſeruant told me you were much diſquieted

Prethee

Prethee loue be not ſo, come walke in,
Ile charm thee with my lute from forth diſturbance.
   Ca. I am not angry ſweet, though if I were,
Thy bright aſpect would ſoone alay my rage;
But my *Maria*, it doth ſomething moue me,
That our friend *Albert* ſo forgets himſelfe.
860   *Ma.* It may be 'ts nothing els, & theres no doubt
Hele ſoone remember his accuſtom'd friendſhip
He thinks, as yet, peraduenture that his preſence
Will but offend, for that our marriage rites
Are but ſo newly paſt.
   Ca. I will ſurmiſe ſo too, and onely thinke,
Some ſerious buſineſſe hinders *Alberts* preſence:
But what ring's that *Maria* on your finger?
   Ma. Tis one you loſt loue, when I did beſtow
A iewell of farre greater worth on you.
870   *Ca.* At what time faireſt?
   Ma. As if you knew not, why dee mak't ſo ſtrange?
   Ca. Yare diſpos'd to riddle, pray lets ſee't,
I partly know it, where waſt you found it?
   Ma. Why in my chamber that moſt gladſome night
When you enricht your loue by my eſcape.
   Ca. How, in your Chamber?
   Ma. Sure *Carracus* I will be angry with you
If you ſeeme ſo forgetfull, I tooke it vp
Then when you left my lodge and went away,
880 Glad of your conqueſt for to ſeeke your friend:
Why ſtand you ſo amaz'd, ſir I hope that kindneſſe
Which then you reaped, doth not preuaile
So in your thoughts, as that you thinke me light.
   Ca. O thinke thy ſelfe *Maria* what thou art:
This is the ring of *Albert* treacherous man,
Hee that enioy'd thy virgin chaſtity:
I neuer did aſcend into thy chamber;
But all that cold night through the frozen field,
Went ſeeking of that wretch, who nere ſought me;
890 But found what his luſt ſought, for deareſt thee.
   Ma, I haue heard enough my *Carracus* to bereaue me of this
little breath, *ſhe ſounds.*   *Ca.*

Ca. All breath be firſt extinguiſht, within there ho?
Enter Nurſe and Seruants.
O Nurſe ſee heere, *Maria* ſaies ſheele die.
Nu. Marry, God forbid, oh M^rif. Ms.Ms. ſhe has breath yet,
ſhees but in a traunce, good ſir take comfort ſheele recouer by
and by.
Ca. No, no, ſheele die Nurſe, for ſhe ſayd ſhe would, an ſhe
had not ſayd ſo, tad bene another matter, but you know Nurſe 900
ſhe nere told a lie, I will beleeue her, for ſhe ſpeaks all truth.
Nur. His memory begins to faile him, come lets beare
This heauy ſpectacle from forth his preſence,
The heauẽs wil lend a hand, I hope, of comfort, *Exeũt Ca.manet.*
Ca. See how they ſteale away my faire *Maria*,
But I will follow after her as farre,
As *Orpheus* did to gaine his ſoules delight,
And *Plutoes* ſelfe ſhall know, although I am not
Skilful in muſique, yet I can be mad,
And force my loues enioyment in deſpight 910
Of hels blacke fury; but ſtay, ſtay *Carracus*,
Where is thy knowledge, and that rational ſence,
Which heauens great Architect indued thee with?
All ſunke beneath the waight of lumpiſh nature?
Are our diuiner parts no noblier free,
Then to be tortur'd by the weake aſſailements
Of earth-ſprung griefes? why is man then accompted
The head commaunder of this vniuerſe,
Next the Creator, when a little ſtorme
Of natures fury ſtraight ore'whelmes his iudgement, 920
But mines no little ſtorme, tis a tempeſt
So full of raging ſelfe-conſuming woe,
That nought but ruine followes expectation:
Oh my *Maria*, what vnheard of ſinne
Haue any of thine Aunceſtors enacted,
That all their ſhame ſhould be powr'd thus on thee;
Or what inceſtuous ſpirit, cruell *Albert*
Left hels vaſt wombe for to enter thee,
And do a miſchiefe of ſuch treachery.
Enter Nurſe weeping. 930
E   Oh

Oh Nurſe, how iſt with *Maria*?
If ere thy tongue did vtter pleaſing words,
Let it now do ſo, or hereafter ere be dumbe in ſorrow.
   Nur. Good ſir take comfort, I am forc't to ſpeake
What will not pleaſe, your chaſte wife ſir is dead.
   Ca. Tis dead indeed, how did you know twas ſo Nurſe?
   Nur. What ſir?
   Ca. That my heart was dead, ſure thou haſt ſerv'd
Dame natures ſelfe, and knoweſt the inward ſecrets
940 Of all our hidden powers, ile loue thee for't;
And if thou wilt teach me that vnknowne skill,
Shalt ſee what wonder *Carracus* will do;
Ile diue into the breaſt of hatefull *Albert*,
And ſee how his blacke ſoule is round incompaſt
By fearefull fiends, oh I would do ſtrange things,
And know to whoſe cauſe Lawyers wil incline,
When they had fees on both ſides, viewe the thoughts
Of for-lorne widdowes when their Knights haue left them;
Search through the guts of greatnes, and behold
950 What ſeueral ſin beſt pleas'd them, thence Ide deſcend
Into the bowels of ſome pocky ſir:
And tell to leachers all the paines he felt,
That they thereby might warned be from luſt,
Troth twill be rare, ile ſtudy it preſently.
   Nur. Alas! hee's diſtracted, what a ſinne
Am I partaker of by telling him,
So curſt an vntruth? But 'twas my Miſtris will
Who is recouer'd, though her griefes neuer
Can be recouer'd, ſhee hath vow'd with teares
960 Her owne perpetuall baniſhment, therefore to him
Death was not more diſpleaſing, then if I
Had told her laſting abſence.
   Ca. I finde my braines too ſhallow farre for ſtudy,
What neede I care for being a Rethmetitian,
Let Cittizens ſonnes ſtand and they will for Ciphers;
Why ſhould I teach them and go beate my braines,
To inſtruct vnapt, and vnconceauing dolts,
And when all's done, my art that ſhould be fam'd,

VVill

VVill by groſſe imitation be but ſham'd,
Your iudgement Madam? 970

  Nur. Good ſir walke in, weele ſend for learned men that
may alay your frenzy.

  Ca. But can *Maria* ſo forget her ſelfe,
As to debarre vs thus of her attendance?

  Nur. Shee is within ſir, pray you wil you walke to her.

  Ca. Oh is ſhe ſo, come then lets ſoftly ſteale
Into her chamber, if ſhe be a ſleepe
Ile laugh ſhalt ſee enough, and thou ſhalt weepe,
Softly good long coate, ſoftly.   *Exeunt.*

Enter Maria *in Pages apparrell.*   III.ii.

  Ma. Ceaſe now thy ſteps *Maria*, and looke backe   981
Vpon that place, where diſtreſt *Carracus*
Hath his ſad being, from whoſe vertuous boſome,
Shame hath conſtrain'd me fly nere to retourne:
I will goe ſeeke ſome vnfrequented path,
Either in deſert woods or wilderneſſe,
There to bewaile my innocent miſhaps,
VVhich heauen hath iuſtly powred downe on me,
In puniſhing my diſobediency.   *Enter young Lo. Wealthy.*
Oh ſee my brother   *Exit Maria.*   990

  Wel. Ho you, three foote and a halfe, why Page I ſay, ſfoot
is vaniſht as ſodainly as a dumbe ſhewe, if a lord had loſt his
way now ſo a had been ſerued, but let me ſee; as I take it, this
is the houſe of *Carracus*, a very faire building, but it lookes as
if twere dead, I can ſee no breath come out of the chimnies;
but I ſhall know the ſtate on't by and by, by the looks of ſome
ſeruing-man: VVhat ho within here?   *Enter Ser.*

  Ser. Good ſir, you haue your armes at liberty, wilt pleaſe
you to with-draw your action of battery.

  Wel. Yes indeed, now you haue made your appearance, is 1000
the liuing-giuer within ſir?

  Ser. You meane my Maſter ſir?

  Wel. You haue hit it ſir, prays'd bee your vnderſtanding, I
am to haue cõference with him, would you admit my preſence.

  Ser. Indeed ſir he is at this time not in health, and may not
be diſturb'd.

E 2   *We.*

We. Sir, an a were in the pangs of childe-bed, I'de ſpeake
with him.   *Enter Carracus.*

Ca. Vpon what cauſe gay-man?

1010 *We*. Sfoote I thinke a be diſturb'd indeed, a ſpeakes more
commaunding then a Conſtable at midnight.
Sir, my lord and father, by me a lord, hath ſent theſe lines in-
clos'd, which ſhew his whole intent.

Ca. Let me peruſe them, if they do portend
To the States good, your anſwere ſhall be ſodaine,
Your entertainement friendly; but if otherwiſe,
Our meaneſt ſubiect ſhall diuide thy greatnes,
You'd beſt looke too 't Embaſſador.

We. Is yous M^r. a Stateſman friend?

1020 *Ser*. Alas no ſir, a vnderſtands not what a ſpeakes.

We. I but when my father dies, I am to be call'd in for one
my ſelfe, and I hope to beare the place as grauely as my ſucceſ-
ſors haue done before me.

Ca. Embaſſador, I finde your Maſters will
Treats to the good of ſomewhat, what it is
You haue your anſwere, and may now depart.

We. I will relate as much ſir, fare ye well.

Ca. But ſtay, I had forgotten quite our chief'ſt affaires,
Your Maſter further writes ſome three lines lower,
1030 Of one *Maria* that is wife to me,
That ſhe and I ſhould trauel now with you
Vnto his preſence.

We. Why now I vnderſtand you ſir, that *Maria* is my ſiſter,
by whoſe coniunction you are created brother, to me a lord.

Ca. But brother lord we cannot goe this iourney.

We. Alas no ſir, we meane to ride it, my ſiſter ſhall ride vpon
my nagge.

Ca. Come then weele in, and ſtriue to woe your ſiſter,
I ha not ſeene her ſir, at leaſt theſe three dayes,
1040 They keepe her in a Chamber, and tell me
Shee's faſt a ſleepe ſtill, you and ile go ſee,

We. Content ſir.

Ser. Mad-men and fooles agree.   *Exennt.*

III.iii.   *Enter Haddit and Rebecka.*

Re.

Re. When you haue got this priſe, you meane to loſe me.

Ha. Nay pree thee doe not thinke ſo, if I doe not marry thee this inſtant night, may I neuer enioy breath a minute after; by heauen I reſpect not his pelfe, thus much, but onely that I may haue wherewith to maintaine thee.

Re. O but to rob my father, though a be bad, the world will 1050 thinke ill of me.

Ha. Thinke ill of thee, can the world pitty him, that nere pittied any, beſides ſince their is no end of his goods, nor beginning of his goodneſſe; had not we as good ſhare his droſſe in his life time, as let Controuerſie and Lawyers deuowre it ats death?

Re. You haue preuail'd, at what houre iſt you entend to haue entrance into his chamber?

Ha. Why iuſt at mid-night, for then our apparition will will ſeeme moſt fearefull, youle make away that we may aſcend vp like ſpirits? 1060

Re. I will, but how many haue you made inſtruments herein?

Ha. Faith none, but my coſen Lightfoote and a plaier.

Re. But may you truſt the player?

Ha. Oh exceeding well, wele giue him a ſpeech a vnder-ſtands not, but now I thinke ont, whats to be done with your Fathers man *Peter*?

Re. Why the leaſt quantity of drinke, will lay him dead a-ſleepe; But harke, I heare my father comming, ſoone in the eue-ning ile conuay you in.

Ha. Till when, let this outward ceremony, be the true pledge 1070 of our inward affections.   *Exit Reb.*

So, this goes better forward then the *Plantation in Virginia*: but ſee here comes halfe the weſt Indies, whoſe rich mines this night I meane to be ranſacking. *Enter Hog, Lightfoote, & Peter.*

Hog. Then youle ſeale for this ſmall Lordſhip you ſay, To morrow your mony ſhall be rightly told vp for you to a peny.

Li. I pray let it, and that your man may ſet contents vpon euerie bag.

Ha. Indeed by that wee may know what we ſteale without labour, for the telling ont ore; how now gent. are ye agreed v- 1080 pon the price of this earth and clay.

Hog, Yes faith Mr. *Haddit* the gent. your friend here makes me paye ſweetlie for't, but let it goe, I hope to inherite hea-

E 3

uen

uen ant be but for doing gentlemen pleaſure.

 Hog. *Peter.*

 Pe. Anon ſir,

 Hogge I wonder how *Haddit* came by that gay ſuite of clothes, all his meanes was conſumed long ſince.

 Pe. Why ſir being vndone himſelfe; a liues by the vndoing
1090 or by-lady, it may be by the doing of others, or peraduenture both a decayed gallant may liue by any thing, if a keepe one thing ſafe.

 Hog. Gentlemen, Ile to the Scriueners to cauſe theſe writings to be drawne.

 Li, Pray doe ſir, weele now leaue you till the morning.

 Hog. Nay, you ſhall ſtay dinner, ile retourne preſently; *Peter* ſome beare here for theſe worſhipful gentlemen.

Exit Hogge, Come *Peter.*

 Ha. We shall be bold no doubt, and that olde penny-father
1100 youle confeſſe by to morrow morning.

 Li. Then his daughter is certainely thine, and condiſcends to all thy wiſhes.

 Had And yet you would not once beleeue it, as if a females fauour could not be obteyn'd by any, but he that weares the Cap of maintenance.

When'ts nothing but acquaintance, and a bold ſpirit,

That may the chiefeſt prize mongſt all of them inherit,

 Li. Well thou haſt got one deſerues the bringing home with trumpets, and fals to thee as miraculouſly as the 1000. pound
1110 did to the Tailor, thanke your good fortune, but muſt Hogges man be made druncke,

 Had. By all meanes: and thus it ſhall be effeȼted, when a comes in with beere, do you vpon ſome ſlight occaſion fall out with him, and if you doe giue him a cuffe or two, it will giue him cauſe to know y'are the more angry, then will I ſlip in and take vp the matter, and ſtriuing to make you two friends, wele make him druncke.

 Li. Its done in conceipt already, ſee where a comes.

Enter Peter.

1120 *Pe.* Wilt pleaſe you to taſt a cup of September beare gentlem.

 Li. Pray begin, wele pleadge you ſir.

Pe.

Pet. Its out ſir, *Li*. then my hand in ſir.　　　(*Li. cuffes him*.

Li. Why goodman hobby horſe, if we out of our gentility offered you to beginne, muſt you out of your raſcality needes take it.

Had. Why how now ſirs, whats the matter.

Pe. The gentleman here fals out with me, vpon nothing in the world but mere courteſie,

Had. By this light but a ſhall not, why Cozen *Lightfoote*.

Pe. Is his name *Lighfoote*, a plague on him, a has a heauie hande.　　　　　　　　　　　*Enter young Lord welthy*. 1130

We. Peace be here: for I came late enough from a madman.

Had. My young Lord, God ſaue you.

We. And you alſo: I could ſpeake it in lattine, but the phraſe is common.

Had. True my Lords, and whats common, ought not much to be dealt with all: but I muſt deſire your helpe my Lord to end a Controuerſie here, betweene this gentleman my friend, and honeſt *Peter*, who I dare beſworne is as ignorant as your Lord-ſhippe. 1140

We. That I will, but my maſters thus much ile ſay vntee, if ſo be this quarrell may be taken vp peaceably, without the in-dangering of my owne perſon, well, and good, otherwiſe I will not meddle therewith, for I haue beene vext late enough al-readie.

Had. Why then my Lord if it pleaſe you, let me, being your inferiour, decree the cauſe betweene them.

We, I doe giue leaue, or permit.

Had. Then thus I will propound a reaſonable motion; how many cuffes *Peter* did this gent. out of his fury make thee parta-ker of? 1150

Pe. Three at the leaſt ſir.

Ha. All which were beſtowed vpon you for beginning firſt *Peter*.

Pe. Yes indeed ſir.

Ha. Why then here the ſentence of your ſuffering, you ſhal both downe into Maſter *Hogs* ſeller *Peter*, and whereas you began firſt to him, ſo ſhall he there to you, and as he gaue you three cuffes, ſo ſhall you retort of in defiance of him, three

blacke

1160 blacke Iackes, which if he deny to pledge; then the glory is
thine, and he accompted by the wiſe diſcretion of my Lord here
a flincher.

    Omnes A very reaſonable motion.

    We. Why ſo, this is better then being among mad-men yet.

    Ha. Were you ſo lately with any my Lord?

    We. Yes faith, Ile tell you all in the Seller, how I was taken
for an Embaſſador, and being no ſooner in the houſe, but the
mad man carries mee vp into the garret for a ſpie, and very
roundly bad me vntruſſe, and had not a courteous ſeruing man
1170 conueied me away whilſt he went to feteh whips I thinke in my
conſcience: not reſpecting my honour a would a breecht me.

    Had. By Lady, and t'was to be fear'd; but come my Lord
wele heare the reſt in the ſeller.

And honeſt *Peter* thou that haſt beene greeued,
My Lord and I, will ſee thee well relieued.   *Exeunt.*

IV.i.   # Actus Quartus.

Enter Albert in the woodes.

How full of ſweet content had this life beene,
If it had beene embraced but before
1180 My burthenous conſcience was ſo fraught with ſinne;
But now my griefes oreſway that happineſſe:
O that ſome lecher or accurſt betrayer
Of ſacred friendſhip, might but here arriue,
And reade the lines repentant on each tree,
That I haue caru'd t'expreſſe my miſery:
My admonitions now, would ſure conuert,
The ſinfulſt creature; I could tell them now,
How idely vaine thoſe humanes ſpend their liues,
That daily grieue not for offences paſt,
1190 But to enioy ſome wantons company;
Which when obteyn'd, what is it, but a blot,
Which their whole liues repentance ſcarſe can cleere:
I could now tell to friend betraying man,
How blacke ſinne is hatefull trechery,
How heauy on their wretched ſoules t'will ſit,

When fearefull death doth plant his ſiege but nere them,
How heauy and affrightfull will their end
Seeme to appeach them, as if then they knew,
The full beginning of their endleſſe woe
VVere then appointed; which aſtoniſhment   1200
O bleſt repentance keepe me *Albert* from
And ſuffer not diſpaire to ouer-whelme,
And make a ſhip-wracke of my heauy ſoule.
    Enter Maria like a page.
Whoſe here, a Page: what blacke diſaſterous fate
Can be ſo cruell to his pleaſing youth?
 Ma. So now *Maria*, here thou muſt forgoe
What nature lent thee to repaie to death;
Famine I thanke thee, I haue found thee kindeſt,
Thou ſet'ſt a period to my miſery.   1210
 Al. It is *Maria* that faire innocent,
Whom my abhorred luſt hath brought to this;
Ile goe for ſuſtenance: and O you powers!
If euer true repentance wan acceptance,
O ſhew it *Albert* now, and let him ſaue
His wronged beauty from vntimely graue. *Exit Albert.*
 Ma. Sure ſome thing ſpake, or els my feebled ſence
Hath loſt the vſe of its due property;
VVhich is more likely, then that in this place,
The voice of humane creature ſhould be heard;   1220
This is farre diſtant from the pathes of men,
Nothing breaths here but wilde and rauening beaſts,
VVith ayry monſters, whoſe ſhaddowing wings doe ſeeme
To taſte a vale of death in wicked liuers;
VVhich I liue dreadleſſe of, and euery hower
Striue to meete death, who ſtill vnkinde auoids me:
But that now gentle famine doth begin
For to giue end to my calamities.
See, here is caru'd vpon this trees ſmooth barke,
Lines knit in verſe, a chaunce farre vnexpcĉted;   1230
Aſſiſt me breath a little to vnfold, what they include.
I that haue writ theſe lines, am one, whoſe ſinne *The Wri-*
Is more then grieuous; for know, that I haue beene *ting*
      F   A brea-

A breaker of my faith, with one whoſe breſt
Was all compos'd of truth: but I digreſt,
And fled, them brats of his deare friendſhips loue,
Claſping to falſhood did a vilane proue,
As thus ſhall be expreſt: my worthy friend
Lou'd a faire beauty, who did condiſcend
1240 In deareſt affeċtion to his vertuous will
He then a night appointed to fulfill
Hymens bleſt-rites, and to conuey away
His loues faire perſon, to which peereleſſe pray
I was acquainted made, and when the hower
Of her eſcape drew on, then luſt did power
Inraged appetite through all my veines,
And baſe deſires in me let looſe the reines
To my licentious will, and that blacke night
When my friend ſhould haue had his chaſt delight,
1250 I fain'd his preſence, and by her, thought him
Rob'd that faire virgin of her honors Iem:
For which moſt heynous, crime vpon each tree
I write this ſtory that mens eyes may ſee,
None but a damn'd one would haue done like me.
Is *Albert* then become ſo penitent,
As in theſe deſarts to deplore his faċts,
Which his vnfain'd repentance ſeemes to cleere:
How good man is, when he laments his ill?
VVho would not pardon now that mans miſdeeds,
1260 Whoſe griefes bewaile them thus, could I now liue,
I'de remit thy fault with *Carracus*:
But death no longer will afford repreeue
Of my aboundant woes: wrong'd *Carracus* farewell,
Liue, and forgiue thy wrongs, for the repentance
Of him that eauſd them, ſo deſerues from thee;
And ſince my eyes do witneſſe *Alberts* griefe,
I pardon *Albert* in my wrongs the chiefe.
Enter Albert like a Hermit.
Alb. How, pardon me, O ſound Angelicall;
1270 But ſee! ſhee faints, O heauens now ſhew your power,
That theſe diſtilled waters made in griefe,

May

May ad ſome comfort to affliction:
Looke vp faire youth, and ſee a remedy.
  Ma. O who diſturbs me, I was hand in hand,
VValking with death vnto the houſe of reſt.
  Al. Let death walke by himſelfe, if a want company,
Theres many thouſands boy, whoſe aged yeeres
Haue tane a ſurfet of earths vanities,
They will goe with him, when he pleaſe to call,
To drinke my boy thy pleaſing tender youth   1280
Cannot deſerue to dye, no, it is for vs,
VVhoſe yeeres are laden by our often ſinnes,
Singing the laſt part of our bleſt repentance,
Are fit for death, and none but ſuch as we,
Death ought to claime; for when a ſnatcheth youth,
It ſhewes him but a tyrant; but when age,
Then is a iuſt, and not compoſ'd of rage.
How fares my lad?
  Ma. Like one imbracing death withall his parts,
Reaching at life but with one little finger;   1290
His minde ſo firmely knit vnto the firſt,
That vnto him the latter ſeemes to be
VVhat may be pointed at, but not poſſeſt.
  Al. O but thou ſhalt poſſeſſe it.
If thou didſt feare thy death but as I doe,
Thou wouldſt take pitty, though not of thy ſelfe,
Yet of my aged yeeres; truſt me my boy,
Tha'ſt ſtrucke ſuch deepe compaſſion in my breaſt,
That all the moiſture which prolongs my life,
VVill from my eyes guſh forth, if now thou leau'ſt me.   1300
  Ma. But can we liue here in this deſart wood,
If not, ile die, for other places ſeeme,
Like tortures to my griefes, may I liue here?
  Alb. I, thou ſhalt liue with me, and I willl tell thee
Such ſtrang occurrents of my fore-paſt life,
That all thy young ſprung griefes ſhall ſeeme but ſparkes
To the great fire of my calamities;
Then ile liue onely with you for to heare,
If any humane woes can be like mine;

F 2

Yet

1310 Yet ſince my being in this darkeſome deſart,
I haue read on trees moſt lamentable ſtories.
    Alb. Tis true indeed, theres one within theſe woods
VVhoſe name is *Albert*, a man ſo full of ſorrow,
That one each tree he paſſeth by he carues,
Such dolefull lines for his raſh follies paſt,
That who ſo reades them, and not drown'd in teares;
Muſt haue a heart fram'd forth of Addamant.
    Ma. And can you helpe to the ſight of him?
    Alb. I when thou wilt, hele often come to me,
1320 And at my Caue ſit a whole winters night,
Recounting of his ſtories, I tell thee boy
Had he offended more then did that man,
VVho ſtole the fire from heauen, his contrition
VVould appeaſe all the gods, and quite reuert
Their wrath to mercy; but come my pretty boy
VVele to my Caue, and after ſome repoſe,
Relate the ſequell of each others woes.   *Exeunt*.

IV.ii.   *Enter Carracus*.
    Ca. What a way haue I come, yet I know not whither,
1330 The ayers ſo cold this winter ſeaſon,
I'me ſure a foole, would any but an aſſe
Leaue a warme matted chamber and a bed,
To run thus in the cold, and which is more,
To ſeeke a woman, a ſlight thing cald woman,
Creatures, with curious nature fram'd as I ſuppoſe,
For rent receauers to her treaſury;
And why I thinke ſo now, Ile giue you inſtance;
Moſt men doe know that natures ſelfe hath made them,
Moſt profitable members, then if ſo,
1340 By often trading in the common wealth
They needs muſt be inricht, why very good,
To whom ought beauty then repaie this gaine
VVhich ſhee by natures gift hath profited;
But vnto nature? why all this I graunt,
VVhy then they ſhall no more be called woman,
For I will ſtile them thus, ſcorning their leaue,
Thoſe that for nature doe much rent receaue.

                                              This

This is a wood ſure, and as I haue read,
In woods are Eccho's which will anſwere men,
To euery queſtion which they do propound: *Echo, Echo, Echo.* 1350
   Ca. O are you there, haue at ye then ifaith,
Echo canſt tell me whether men or women
Are for the moſt part damb'd? *Echo* moſt part damb'd.
   Ca. Of both indeed, how true this Echo ſpeakes,
Echo, now tel me if mongſt 1000. women,
There be one chaſte, or none? *Echo*, none.
   Ca. Why ſo I thinke, better and better ſtill:
Now further Echo, in a world of men,
Is there one faithfull to his friend, or no?   *Echo* no.
   Ca. Thou ſpeak'ſt moſt true, for I haue found it ſo;   1360
Who ſayd thou waſt a woman Echo lies,
Thou couldſt not then anſwere ſo much of truth,
Once more good Echo,
Was my *Maria* falſe by her owne deſire,
Or waſt againſt her will?   *Echo* againſt her wil.
Troth 't may be ſo, but canſt thou tell,
Whether ſhe be dead or not?   *Echo* not.
   Ca. Not dead. *Echo* not dead.
Then without queſtion ſhe doth ſurely liue: But I do trouble
thee too much, therfore good ſpeak truth, farewel. *Ec.* farewel. 1370
   Ca. How quick it anſwers, ô that Conncellors
Would thus refolue mens doubts without a fee.
How many country Clyents then might reſt
Free from vndooing, no plodding pleader then
Would purchaſe great poſſeſſions with his tongue;
Were I ſome demy-god, or had that power,
I'de ſtraight make this Echo here a iudge;
Hee'd ſpend his iudgement in the open court,
As now to me, without being once ſolicited
In's priuate chamber, tis not bribes could win   1380
Him to o're-ſway mens right, nor could he be
Lead to damnation for a little pelfe;
He would not harbour malice in his heart,
Or enuious hatred, baſe diſpight or grudge,
But be an vpright, iuſt, and equall Iudge:

F 3

But

But now imagine that I ſhould confront
Treacherous *Albert*, who hath rais'd my front.
But I feare this idle prate hath
Made me quite forget my *cinque pace*. *he daunceth.*
Enter Albert.

1390   *Alb*. I heard the Eccho anſwere vnto one,
That by his ſpeech cannot be far remote
From of this ground, and ſee I haue diſcried him:
Oh heauens! its *Carracus*, whoſe reaſons ſeate
Is now vſurpt by madnes, and diſtraction;
Which I the author of confuſion
Haue planted here, by my accurſed deeds.
    Ca. O are you come ſir, I was ſending the Tauerne-boy for
ye, I haue been practiſing here, and can do none of my loftie
1400 trickes.
    Alb. Good ſir, if any ſparke do yet remaine
Of your conſumed reaſon, let me ſtriue.
    Ca. To blow it out, troth I moſt kindly thank you,
Heres friendſhip to the life; but father whay-beard,
Why ſhould you thinke me void of reaſons fire,
My youthfull dayes being in the height of knowledge?
I muſt confeſſe your old yeeres gaines experience;
But that's ſo much orer-ul'd by dotage,
That what you think experience ſhall effect,
1410 Short memory deſtroies, what ſay you now ſir?
Am I mad now, that can anſwere thus
To all intergatories?
    Alb. But though your words do ſauor ſir of iudgement,
Yet when they derogate from the due obſeruance
Of fitting times, they ought not be reſpected,
No more, then if a man ſhould tell a tale
Of fained mirth in midſt of extreame ſorrowes.
    Ca. How did you know my ſorrowes ſir?
What though I haue loſt a wife,
1420 Muſt I be therefore grieued; am I not happy
To be ſo freed of a continuall trouble?
Had many a man ſuch fortune as I,
In what a heauen would they thinke themſelues?

Being

Being releaſt of all thoſe threatning cloudes,
Which in the angry skies, cal'd womens browes,
Sit euer menacing tempeſtuous ſtormes:
But yet I needs muſt tell you, old December,
My wife was cleere of this; within her browe,
Sh'ad not a wrinkle nor a ſtorming frowne;
But like a ſmooth well poliſht Iuory,   1430
It ſeem'd ſo pleaſant to the looker on,
She was ſo kinde, of nature ſo gentle,
That if ſh'ad done a fault ſhee'd ſtraight go die for't:
Was not ſhe then a rare one?
What weep'ſt thou aged *Neſtor*?
Take comfort man, *Troy* was ordain'd by fate
To yeeld to vs, which we will ruinate.
     Alb. Good ſir walke with me, but where you ſee
The ſhaddowing Elmes, within whoſe circling round
There is a holy ſpring about incompaſt,   1440
By dandling ſiccamores and violets,
Whoſe waters cure all humane maladies:
Few drops thereof being ſprinkled on your temples,
Reuiues your fading memory, and reſtores
Your ſences loſt vnto their perfect being.
     Ca. Is it cleere water ſir, and very freſh?
For I am thirſty; giues it a better relliſh
Then a cup of dead wine with flies in't?
     Alb. Moſt pleaſant to the taſte, pray will you goe.
Ca. Faſter then you I beleeue ſir.   *Exeunt*.   1450
                Enter Maria.   IV.iii.
     Ma. I am walkt forth from my preſeruers caue,
To ſearch about theſe woods, only to ſee
The penitent *Albert*, whoſe repentant minde
Each ttee expreſſeth: ô that ſome power diuine
Would hither ſend my vertuous *Carracus*;
Not for my owne content, but that he might
See how his diſtreſt friend repents the wrong,
Which his raſh folly, moſt vnfortunate
Acted against him and me, which I forgiue   1460
A hundred times a day, for that more often

                        My

My eyes are witnes to his ſaid complaints,
How the good Hermit ſeemes to ſhare his mones,
Which in the day time he deplores 'mongſt trees,
And in the night his Caue is fild with ſighs;
No other bed doth his weake limbs ſupport
Then the cold earth, no other harmony
To rocke his cares aſleepe, but bluſtering windes,
Or ſome ſwift Current, headlong ruſhing downe
1470 From a high Mountaines top, powring his force
Into the Oceans gulfe, where being ſwallowed,
Seemes to bewaile his fall with hideous words:
No other ſuſtentation to ſuffice
What Nature claimes, but rawe vnſauowry rootes,
With troubled waters, where vntamed beaſts,
Do bathe themſelues:
   Enter Satyrs, dance & Exeunt.
Ay me! what things are theſe?
What pretty harmeleſſe things they ſeeme to be?
1480 As if delight had no where made abode,
But in their nimble ſport. *Enter Albert.*
Yonders the courteous Hermit, and with him
Albert it ſeeemes, ô ſee tis *Carracus,*
Ioy do not now confound me.
 Ca. Thanks vnto heauens & thee thou holy man,
I haue attain'd what doth adorne mans being,
That pretious Iemme of reaſon, by which ſoly,
We are diſcern'd from rude and brutiſh beaſts,
No other difference being twixt vs and them.
1490 How to repay this more then earthly kindneſſe,
Lies not within my power, but in his
That hath indu'd thee with celeſtiall gifts,
To whom Ile pray, he may beſtow on thee
What thou deſerv'ſt, bleſt immortality.
 Alb. Which vnto you befall, thereof moſt worthy:
But vertuous ſir, what I will now requeſt
From your true generous nature, is, that you would
Be pleas'd to pardon that repentant Wight
Whoſe ſinfull ſtories vpon you trees barke,

Your

Your ſelfe did reade, for that you ſay, to you   1500
Thoſe wrongs were done.
   Ca. Indeed they were, and to, a deere wife loſt;
Yet I forgiue him, as I wiſh the heauens
May pardon me.
   Ma. So doth *Maria* to.   *ſhe diſcouers her ſelfe.*
   Ca. Liues my *Maria* then? what gratious plannet
Gaue thee ſafe conduct to theſe deſert woods?
   Ma. My late miſhap (repented now by all,
And therfore pardon'd) compelled me to fly,
Where I had periſhed for want of foode,   1510
Had not this courteous man awak't my ſence,
In which, deaths ſelfe had partly intereſt.
   Ca. Alas *Maria*! I am ſo farre indebted
To him already, for the late recouery of
My owne weakneſſe, that tis impoſsible
For vs to attribute ſufficient thankes,
For ſuch aboundant good.
   Alb. I rather ought to thanke the heauens Creator,
That he vouchſaf't me ſuch eſpeciall grace,
In dooing ſo ſmall a good, which could I howerly   1520
Beſtowe on all, yet could I not aſſwage
The ſwelling rancor of my fore-paſt crimes.
   Ca. O ſir, diſpaire not for your courſe of life
(were your ſinnes farre more odious then they be)
Doth moue compaſsion and pure clemency
In the al-ruling Iudge, whoſe powerfull mercy
Oreſwayes his iuſtice, and extends it ſelfe
To all repentant mindes, hee's happier farre
That ſinnes, and can repent him of his ſinne;
Then the ſelfe iuſtifier, who doth ſurmiſe   1530
By his owne workes to gaine ſaluation,
Seeming to reach at heauen and claſpe damnation:
You then are happy, and our penitent friend,
To whoſe wiſht preſence pleaſe you now to bring vs,
That in our gladſome armes we infold
His much eſteemed perſon, and forgiue
The iniuries of his raſh follies paſt.
G

Alb.

Alb. Then ſee falſe *Albert* proſtrate at your feete,
               he diſcouers himſelfe.
1540 Deſiring Iuſtice for his haynous ill.
    Ca. Is it you *Alberts* ſelfe that hath preſerv'd vs?
O bleſt bewailer of thy miſery!
    Ma. And woful'ſt liuer in calamity.
    Ca. From which, right worthy friend, its now high time
You be releaſt, come then you ſhall with vs,
Our firſt and chiefeſt welcome my *Maria*,
We ſhall receaue at your good fathers houſe;
Who, as I do remember, in my frenzy
Sent a kinde letter which deſired our preſence.
1550   *Alb.* So pleaſe you, vertuous paire, *Albert* will ſtay,
And ſpend the remnant of this weary-ſome life
In theſe darke woods.
    Ca. Then you neglect the comforts heauen doth ſend,
To your abode on earth, if you ſtay here
Your life may end in torture, by the cruelty
Of ſome wilde rauenous beaſts, but if mongſt men
When you depart, the faithfull prayers of many
Will much auaile, to crowne your ſoule with bliſſe.
    Alb. Lou'd *Carracus*, I haue found in thy conuerſe
1560 Comfort ſo bleſt, that nothing now but death,
Shall cauſe a ſeparation in our being.
    Ma. Which heauen confirme.
    Ca. Thus by the breach of faith, our friendſhips knit
In ſtronger bonds of loue.
    Alb. Heauen ſo continue it.   *Exeunt.*

V.i.   # Actus Quintus.

Enter Hogge *in his chamber with* Rebecka *laying downe his
bed, and ſeeming to put the keyes vnder his boulſter
conuayeth them into her pocket.*

1570   *Ho* So, haue you layd the keyes of the outward dores vnder
my boulſter?   *Re.* Yes forſooth.
    Ho. Go your way to bed then.   *Exit Re.*
                              I won-

I wonder who did at the ſirſt inuent
Theſe beds, the breeders of diſeaſe and ſloth,
A was no ſouldier ſure, nor no ſcholler,
And yet a might be vety well a Courtier;
For no good husband would haue bin ſo idle,
No Vſurer neither; yet here the bed affords   *diſcouers his gold.*
Store of ſweet golden ſlumbers vnto him;
Here ſleepes commaund in warre, *Cæſar* by this   1580
Obtain'd his triumphs, this will fight mans cauſe,
When fathers, brethren, and the neer'ſt of friends
Leaues to aſsiſt him, all content to this
Is meerely vaine, the louers whoſe affections
Do ſimpathize together in full pleaſure,
Debarr'd of this their ſummer ſodaine ends,
And care the winter to their former ioyes,
Breath's ſuch a cold blaſt on their Turtles bils;
Hauing not this, to ſhrow'd him forth his ſtormes,
They ſtraight are forc't to make a ſeparation,   1590
And ſo liue vnder thoſe that rule ore this.
The Gallant, whoſe illuſtrious out-ſide drawes
The eyes of wantons to behold with wonder
Hir rare ſhap't parts, for ſo he thinks they be,
Deck't in the roabes of gliſtering gallantry:
Hauing not this, attendant on his perſon,
Walkes with a clowdy brow, and ſeemes to all
A great contemner of ſociety;
Not for the hate he beares to company,
But for the want of this ability: 1600
O ſiluer! thou that art the baſeſt captiue
Kept in this priſon: how many pale offendors
For thee haue ſuffered ruine; but ô my gold
Thy ſight's more pleaſing, then the ſeemely locks
Of yellow hair'd *Apollo*, and thy touch
More ſmooth and dainty, then the downe-ſoft white
Of Ladies tempting breaſt, thy bright aſpect
Dimm's the great'ſt luſter of heauens Waggoner.
But why goe I about to extoll thy worth,
Knowing that Poets cannot compaſſe it;   1610

G 2   But

But now giue place my gold for heres a power
Of greater glory and fupremacy
Obfcures thy being, here fits enthroniz'd
The fparkling diamond, whofe bright reflection
Cafts fuch a fplendor on thefe other Iemmes,
Mongft which he fo maiefticall appeares,   *A flafh of fire and*
As if—now my good angels guard me.   *Lightfoote afcends*
    Li. Melior vigilantia fomno.   *like a fpirit.*
Stand not amaz'd good man, for what appeares
1620 fhall adde to thy content, be voide of feares,
I am the fhaddow of rich Kingly *Creffus*,
Sent by his greatnes from the lower world
To make thee mighty, and to fway on earth
By thy aboundant ftore, as he himfelfe doth
In *Elizium*; how he raigneth there,
His fhaddow will vnfold, giue thou then eare.
In Vnder-ayre where faire *Elizum* ftands
Beyond the riuer ftiled *Acharon*,
He hath a Caftle built of Adamant;
1630 Not fram'd by vaine enchauntment, but there fixt,
By the all burning hands of warlike fpirits,
Whofe windowes are compos'd of pureft chriftall,
And deckt within with orientall pearles:
There the great fpirit of *Creffus* royall felfe,
Keepes his abode in ioyous happineffe;
He is not tortur'd there as Poets feine
With molten gold and fulphrie flames of fire,
Or any fuch molefting perturbation;
But there reputed as a demy-god,
1640 Feafting with *Pluto* and his *Proferpine*,
Night after night with all delicious cates,
With greater glory then feauen kingdomes ftates.
Now further know the caufe of my appearance,
The kingly *Creffus* hauing by fames trumpe,
Heard that thy lov'd defires ftand affected
To the obtaining of aboundant wealth,
Sends me his fhade, thus much to fignifie,
That if thou wilt become famous on earth,

Heele

Heele giue to thee euen more then infinite;
And after death with him thou ſhalt pertake   1650
The rare delights beyond the ſtigian lake.
   Hog. Great *Creſſus* ſhaddow may diſpoſe of me to what hee
pleaſeth.
   Li. So ſpeakes obediency.
For which ile raiſe thy lowly thoughts as high,
As *Creſſus* were in his mortality;
Stand then vndaunted whil'ſt I raiſe thoſe ſpirits,
By whoſe laborious taske and induſtry,
Thy treaſure ſhall abound and multiply.

Aſcend Aſcarion thou that art a powerfull ſpirit and doſt con-   1660
    uert ſiluer to gold, I ſay aſcend and one me Creſus ſhade at-
    tend to worke the pleaſure of his will.
                       the Player appeares.
Pla. What would then *Creſus* liſt to fill
Some mortals cofers vp with gold,
Chaunging the ſiluer it doth hold:
By that pure mettle ift be ſo,
By the infernall gates I ſweare,
Where Radamanth doth dominere:
By *Creſus* name and by his caſtle,   1670
Where winter nights he keepeth waſſell;
By Demogorgon and the fates,
And by all theſe low country ſtates;
That after knowledge of thy minde,
Aſcarion like the ſwift pac't winde,
Will flye to finiſh thy commaund.
   Li. Take then this ſiluer out of hand,
And beare it to the Riuer *Tagus*,
Beyond th'aboade of *Archi Magus*;
Whoſe golden ſands vpon it caſt,   1680
Transforme it into gold at laſt:
Which being effected ſtraight retourne,
And ſuddaine too, or I will ſpurne
This truncke of thine into the pit,
Where all the helliſh furies ſit,
            G 3   Scrat-

Scratching their eyes out quicke begon.

    Pla. Swifter in courſe then doth the Sunne. *Exit player.*

    Li. How fair'ſt thou mortall be? not terrified

At theſe infernall motions, know that ſhortly

1690 Great *Creſſus* ghoſt ſhall in the loue he beares thee,

Giue thee ſufficient power by thy owne worth,

To raiſe ſuch ſpirits.

    Hog. Creſſus is much too liberall in his fauour,

To one ſo farre deſertleſſe as poore *Hog.*

    Li. Poore *Hogge,* O ſpeake not that word poore againe,

Leaſt the whole apletree of *Creſſus* bounty,

Crackt into ſhiuers ouerthrow thy fortunes,

For he abhorres the name of pouerty,

And will grow ſicke to heare it ſpoke by thoſe,

1700 VVhom he intends to raiſe; but ſee the twi-light

Poſteth before the Charriot of the Sunne,

Brings word of his approch:

VVe muſt be ſuddaine, and with ſpeed raiſe vp

The ſpirit *Bazan*: that can ſtraight transforme

Gold into pearle; be ſtill and circumſpect.

Bazon aſcend vp from the treaſure of Pluto, *where thou did'ſt at*
      pleaſure metamorphiſe all his gold into pearle, which boue
      a thouſand folde exceeds the valew, quickly riſe to Creſus
      ſhade, who hath a priſe to be performed by thy ſtrength.

1710   *Bazon aſcends.*

Bazon I am no Fencer, yet at length

From *Plutoes* preſence and the Hall,

VVhere *Proſerpine* keepes feſtiuall,

I'me hether come and now I ſee,

To what intent 'Ime rai'ſd by thee;

It is to make that mortall rich,

That at his fame mens eares may itch;

VVhen they doe heare but of his ſtore,

He hath one daughter and no more;

1720 VVhich all the lower powers decree,

Shee to one *Wealthy* wedded be;

By which coniunction there ſhall ſpring,

Young heires to *Hogge* whereon to fling:

His maſſe of treaſure when a dies,

Thus

Thus *Bazon* truely propheſies:
But come my taske I long to reare,
His fame aboue the Hemy-ſpheare.
    Li. Take then the gould which here doth lie,
And quicke retourne it by and by;
All in choiſe pearle whither to goe,   1730
I need not tell you, for you know.
    Ha. Indeed I doe, and *Hogge* ſhall finde it ſo.   *Exit Had.*
    Li. Now mortall there is nothing doth remaine,
Twixt thee and thine aboundance, onely this
Turne thy eyes weſtward, for from thence appeareth
Aſcarion with thy gould, which hauing brought
And at thy foote ſurrendred, make obeyſance;
Then turne about and fix thy tapers weſtward,
From whence great *Bazon* brings thy orient pearle;
VVho'le lay it at thy feet much like the former.   1740
    Hog. Then I muſt make to him obeyſance thus.
    Li. VVhy ſo, in meane time *Creſſus* ſhadewill reſt
Vpon thy bed, but aboue all take heed,
You ſuffer not your eies to ſtray aſide,
From the direct point I haue ſet thee at:
For though the ſpirit do delay the time,
And not retourne your treaſure ſpeedily.
    Hog. Let the loſſe light on me, if I neglect
I ouerſlip what *Creſſus* ſuit commaunde.
    Lo. So now practiſe ſtanding, though it be nothing agreea- 1750
ble to your hogs age, let me ſee among theſe writings is my ne-
phew *Haddits* mortgage; but in taking that it may breed ſuſ-
pect on vs, wherefore this boxe of Iewels will ſtand farre better
and let that alone, it is now breake of day, and nere by this the
marriage is confirm'd betwixt my Coſen & great *Creſſus* friends
daughter here, whom I would now leaue to his moſt weighty
So gentle ſir adue, time not permits   (cogitations.
To heare thoſe paſſions and thoſe franticke fits;
Your ſubiect to when you ſhall find how true,
Grear *Creſſus* ſhade hath made an aſſe of you.   1760
    Hog. Let me now ruminate to my ſelfe why *Creſſus* ſhould
be ſo great a fauorer to me, & yet to what end ſhould I deſire to
                                       know

know I thinke it is ſufficient, it is ſo, and I would a had beene
ſo ſooner, for he and his ſpirits would haue ſaued me much labour in the purchaſing of wealth; but then indeed it would haue
beene the confuſion of 2. or 3. Scriueners, which by my meanes
haue beene properly rais'd: but now imagine this onely a tricke
whereby I may be guld; but how can that be? are not my dores
lockt, haue I not ſeene with my owne eyes the aſcending of the
1770 ſpirits? haue I not heard with my owne eares the inuocations
wherewith they were rais'd? could any but ſpirits appeare
through ſo firme a floore as this is? tis impoſſible: But harke, I
heare the ſpirit *Aſcarion* comming with my gould, O bountiful
Creſſus; Ile build a temple to thy mightineſſe.

Enter young Lo. Welthy and Peter.

We. O *Peter*, how long haue we ſlept vpon the hogſhead?

Pe. I thinke a doſen howers my Lord, and tis nothing, Ile
vndertake to ſleepe ſixteene, vpon the receipt of two cups of
muskadine.

1780 *We.* I maruell what's become of *Haddit* and *Lighfoote*?

Pe. Hang'em flinchers they ſluncke away as ſoone as they
had druncke as much as they were able to carry, which no generous ſpirit would a done in deed.

We. Yet I beleeue *Had.* had his part, for to my thinking the
ſeller went round with him when a left vs, but are we come to a
bed yet? I muſt needs ſleepe.

Pe. Come ſoftly by any meanes, for we are now vpon the
threſhold of my maſters chamber, through which ile bring you
to Miſtris *Rebeckaes* lodging, giue me your hand and come very
1790 nicely.   (*Peter fals into the hole.*

We. Where art *Peter.*   —*Pe.*—O oh o.

We. Wheres this noyſe *Peter* canſt tell?

Hog, I heare the voice of my adopted ſonne in law.

We. Why *Peter* wilt not anſwere me?

Pe. O my Lord aboue, ſtand ſtill, I am falne downe at leaſt
30. fathome deepe, if you ſtand not ſtill till I recouer and haue
lighten a candle, y'are but a dead man.

Hog. I am rob'd, I am vndone, I am deluded, whoſe in my
chamber?

We. Tis

We. Tis I, the Lord your ſonne that ſhall be, vpon my honor   1800
I came not to rob you.

Hog. I ſhall run mad, I ſhall run mad.

Wel. Why then tis my fortune to be terrifide with madmen.

Enter Peter with a candle.

Pe: Where are you my Lord?

Hog. Here my Lady? where are you rogue when theeues
breake into my houſe?

Pe. Breaking my necke in your ſeruice a plague ont.

We. But are you rob'd indeed father *Hogge*, of how much I
praye?   1810

Hog. Of all, of all; ſee here, they haue left me nothing but 2.
or 3. roles of parchment, here they came vp like ſpirits, & tooke
my ſiluer, gold, and Iewels; wheres my daughter?

Pe. Shees not in the houſe ſir? the ſtreete doores are wide
open.

We. Nay tis no matter where ſhee is now? ſhele ſcarce be
worth a 1000. pound and thats but a taylors priſe.

Ho. Then youle not haue her ſir?

We. No as I hope to liue in peace.

Hog. Why bee't ſo, bee't ſo, confuſion cannot come in a   1820
more fitter time on all of vs: O bountifull *Creſſus*, how fine thy
ſhaddow hath deuoured my ſubſtance.

Pe. Good my Lord promiſe him to marry his daughter, or a
will be mad preſently, though you neuer intend to haue her.

We. Well father *Hogge*, though you are vndone, your
daughter ſhall not be, ſo long as a Lords can ſtand her in any
ſtead: come you ſhall with me to my Lord and father, whoſe
warrants wee will haue for the apprehending of all ſuſpitious
liues, and though the labour be infinite, you muſt conſider your
loſſe is ſo.   1830

Hog. Come, ile doe any thing to gaine my golde.

Pe. Till which be had, my fare will be but cold.   *Exeunt.*

Enter Haddit, Reb. Lightfoote, and Prieſt.   V.ii.

Had. Now Mr. Parſon we will no further trouble you, and
for the tying of our true loue knot, heres a ſmall amends.

Prie. Tis more then due ſir, yet ile take it all,
Should kindneſſe be diſpis'd, good will would fall.

H

Vnto

Vnto a lower ebbe, ſhould we deteſt
The gratefull giuers gift, *Verisſimo eſt.*
1840   *Had.* It's true indeed, good morrow honeſt Parſon.
    Pe. Yet if you pleaſe, ſir *Iohn* will backe ſurrender
The ouerplus of what you now did tender.
    Ha. O by no meanes, I pree thee friend, good-morrow.
    Li. Why if you pleaſe Sir *Iohn* to me reſtore,
The ouerplus ile giue it to the poore.
    Pe. O pardon ſir, for by our worſhips leaue,
We ought to giue from whence we doe receaue.
    Had. VVhy then to me ſir *Iohn.*
    Pri. To all a kinde good morrow.   *Exit Prieſt.*
1850   *Ha.* A moſt fine Vicar, there was no other meanes to be rid
of him: but why are you ſo ſad *Rebecka?*
    Re. To thinke in what eſtate my father is?
VVhen he beholds that he is meerely guld.
    Had. Nay be not grieu'd, for that which ſhould rather giue
you cauſe of content, for 'twill be a meanes to make him abandon his auarice, and ſaue a ſoule almoſt incurable: but now to
our owne affaires, this marriage of ours muſt not yet be known
leaſt it breed ſuſpition, we will bring you *Rebecka* vnto *Atlas*
his houſe, whil'ſt we two goe vnto the old Lord *Welthies*, hauing
1860 ſome acquaintance with his ſonne in law *Carracus,* who I vnderſtand is there, where no queſtion but we ſhall finde your father proclaiming his loſſe, thether you ſhall come ſome what
after vs, as it were to ſeeke him, where I doubt not but ſo to or-
der the matter, that I will receaue you as my wife, from his own
hands.
    Re. May it ſo happy proue.
    Li. Amen ſay I, for ſhould our laſt tricke be knowne, great
Creſſus ſhade would haue a coniured time ont.
    Had. Tis true, his Caſtle of Addamant would ſcarce holde
1870 him: but come this will be good cauſe for laughter heteafter.
Then wele relate how this great bird was puld,
Of his rich fethers, and moſt finely guld.   *Exeunt.*
V. iii.   *Enter old Lo. Welthy, with Car. Ma. and Albert.*
    Lo. More welcome *Carracus,* then friendly truce

To

To a beſieged Citty all diſtreſt;
How early this glad morning are you come
To make me happy, for pardon of your offence
I'ue giuen a bleſſing, which may heauen confirme,
In trebble manner on your vertuous liues.
And may our liues and duty daily ſtriue,   1880
To be found worthy of that louing fauour,
Which from your reuerent age we now receaue,
Without deſert, or merrit.   *Enter young Wel. Hogge & Peter.*
   We. Roome for a deſirer of Iuſtice, what my ſiſter *Maria*;
Who thought to haue met you here?
   Ma. You may ſee brother, vnlook't for gueſts proofe of-
ten troubleſome.
   We. Well, but is your husband there any quieter then a was?
   Ca. Sir, I muſt deſire you to forget all iniuries, if, in not be-
ing my ſelfe, I offered you any.   1890
   Alb. Ile ſee that peace concluded.
   We. Which I agree to, for patience is a vertue father Hogge.
   Ho. Was it you ſonne that cride ſo loud for iuſtice?
   We. Yes marry was it, and this the party to whome it apper-
taines.
   Ho. O my moſt honored lord I am vndone, rob'd this black
night of all the wealth and treaſure, which theſe many yeeres I
haue howerly labored for.
   Lo. And who are thoſe haue done this outrage to you?
   Ho. Oh knew I that, I then my lord were happy.   1900
   Lo. Come you for Iuſtice then, not knowing 'gainſt whom
the courſe of Iuſtice ſhould extend it ſelfe?
Nor yet ſuſpe&ct; you none?
   Ho. None but the diuell.
   We. I thought a was a Cheater, ere ſince I heard two or three
Templers ſweare at dice the laſt Chriſtmas, that the diuel had
got all.   *Enter Haddit and Lightfoote.*
   Ha. My kinde acquaintance, Ioy to thy good ſucceſſe.
   Ca. Noble, and free-borne *Haddit*, welcome.
   Li. M^r. *Hogge* good-day.   1910
   Ho. For I haue had a bad night on't
   Li. Sickneſſe is incident to age, what be the writings ready

H 2

to

to be ſealed, wee intreated laſt day.

Ho. Yes I thinke they are, would the Scriuiner were paid for the making them.

Li. A ſhalbe ſo, though I doote my ſelfe, is the mony put vp as I appointed?

Ho. Yes tis put vp, confuſion ceaſe the receiuers.

Li. Heauen bleſſe vs all, what meane you ſir?

Ho. O ſir, I was robb'd this night of all I had, My daughter to is loſt, and I vndone.

Li. Marry, God forbid, after what manner I pray.

Ho. O to recount ſir will breede more ruth, Then did the tale of that high Troian Duke, To the ſad fated Carthagenian Queene.

Ha. What exclamations that?

Li. What you will grieue at Coze, Your worſhipfull friend M. Hogge is robb'd.

Ha. Rob'd, by whom or how?

Li. O theres the griefe, a knowes not whome to ſuſpect.

Ha. The feare of hell oretake them whatſoere they be: but wheres your daughter, I hope ſhe is ſafe.   *Enter Re.*

Ho. Thankes heauen, I ſee ſhee's now ſo, where haſt thou been my girle?

Re. Alas ſir, carried by amazemẽt, I know not where, purſu'd by the robbers forc't to fly as mad affright, through al the City ſtreets to ſeek redreſſe, but that lay faſt aſleepe in all mens hou-ſes, nor would lend an eare to the diſtreſt.

Ha. O heauy accident, but ſee you grieue too much, Being your daughter's found, for th'other loſſe; Since tis the will of heauen to giue and take, Value it as nothing, you haue yet ſufficient To liue in bleſt content, had you no more But my ſmall mortgage for your daughter here; Whom I haue euer lov'd in deer'ſt affection, If ſo you pleaſe ſo much to fauour me, I will accept her ſpight of pouerty, And make her iointure of ſome ſtore of land, Which by the loſſe of a good aged friend Late fell to me, what iſt a match or no.   *Ho.* It is.

Then

Then Ile haue witneſſe on't, my lord and gent.
Pleaſe you draw neere, to be here witneſſes
To a wiſht contract, twixt this maid and I.
   Omnes We all are willing.
   Ho. Then in the preſence of you all, I giue my daughter free-
ly to this gent. as wife, and to ſhew how much I ſtand affected
to him for dowry with her, I doe backe reſtore his mortgag'd
lands, and for their loues I vowe, euer hereafter to deteſt, re-
nounce, loath and abhorre all ſlauiſh auarice:
Which doth aſcend from hell, ſent by the diuell,   1960
To be 'mongſt men the actor of all euill.
   Om. A bleſt conuerſion.
   Lo. A good far vnexpected, and now gentlemen,
I do enuite you all to feaſt with me
This happy day, that we may altogether
Applaud his good ſucceſſe, and let this day be ſpent,
In ſports and ſhewes with gladſome merriment:
Come bleſt conuerted man wcele lead the way,
As vnto heauen I hope we ſhall.
   Ho. Heauen graunt we may.   1970
   Ca. Come my *Maria* and repent nt friend,
Wee three haue taſted worſt of miſery,
Which now adde ioy to our felicity.
   Ha. We three are happy wee haue gain'd much wealth,
And though we haue done it by a tricke of ſtealth,
Yet all I truſt are pleas'd, and will our ill acquite,
Since it hath ſau'd a ſoule was hells by right.
   We. To follow after then, our lot doth fall,
Now rime it *Peter.*
   Pe. A good night to all.   *Exeunt omnes.*   1980

FINIS.

EPILOGVE.

NOW *expectation hath at full receiued*
  What we late promised, if in ought we haue pleased,
  Tis all vve sought to accomplish, and much more
Then our vveake merrit dares to attribute
Vnto it selfe, till you vouchsafe to dayne
In your kinde censure, so to gratifie
Our triuiall labours:———
If it hath pleased the iudiciall eare,
Wee haue our Authors wish, and void of feare
Dare ignorant men, to shew their worst of hate.
It not detracts, but adds vnto that state
Where desert florisheth.
Weele rest applouded in their derogation,
Though with an hisse they crowne that confirmation:
For this our Author saith, ift proue distastfull,
He onely grieues you spent two houres so wast-full:
But if it like, and you affect his pen,
You may commaund it when you please agen.